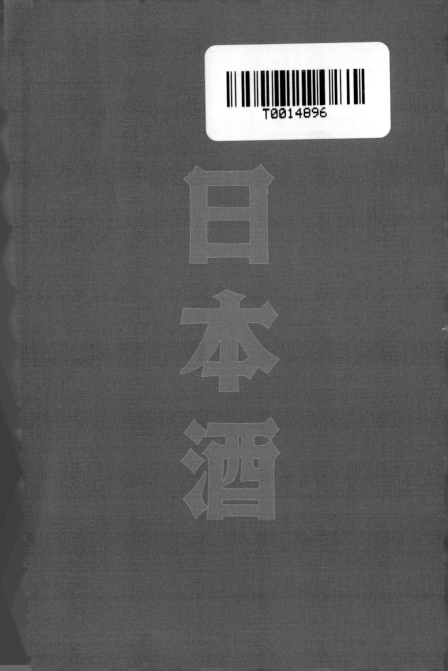

日本酒

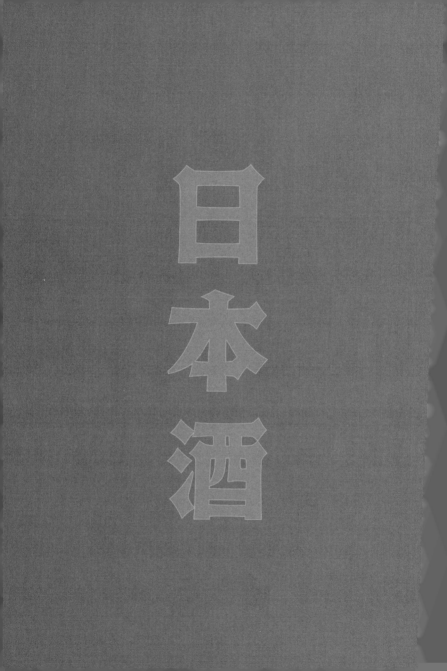

日本酒

DISCOVERING
Yamaguchi
Sake

DISCOVERING
Yamaguchi Sake

A Taster's Guide to
BREWERIES,
CULTURE,
& TERRAIN

Jim Rion

Foreword by Melinda Joe

Stone Bridge Press • *Berkeley, California*

Published by
Stone Bridge Press
P. O. Box 8208, Berkeley, CA 94707
sbp@stonebridge.com • www.stonebridge.com

Translation of excerpt from Santoka's *Travel Journals* by the author. Portions of the section "Yamagata Honten" adapted and updated from an article originally published in *Sake Today* #22 (Summer 2019). Portions of "Nagayama Honke Shuzojo" previously appeared on Nippon.com in the article "Terroir Japonais: Japan's Sake Meets France's 'Vin Naturel' Philosophy." Portions of "Connections—Ceramic Artists" previously appeared on Nippon.com in the article "Today's Hagiyaki: Traditional Craft Encounters High Art."

Image on front cover, title page, and page 19: "Motonosumi Inari Shrine in Yamaguchi Prefecture" from BigStock, ©SeanPavonePhoto. Sake labels on front cover and interior used with permission of their respective breweries. Photos on following pages provided by the breweries: Murashige Shuzo, page 51; Nakashimaya Shuzojo, page 83; Ohmine Shuzo, page 153; Okazaki Shuzo, page 186; Sakai Shuzo, page 57; Shimonoseki Shuzo, page 141; Shintani Shuzo, page 113; Sumikawa Shuzo, page 191; Yachiyo Shuzo, page 198; Yamagata Honten, page 90; Yaoshin Shuzo, page 63. Photo of Abu no Tsuru Shuzo, page 169, © OUWN Co. LTD. All other photos belong to the author unless otherwise noted.

All maps created by the author using the free service by CraftMAP: http://www.craftmap.box-i.net.

10 9 8 7 6 5 4 3 2 1   2026 2025 2024 2023

p-ISBN 978-1-61172-080-8
e-ISBN 978-1-61172-960-3

Contents

Foreword   7
Preface   9
Sake Terms and Classifications   13

The Yamaguchi Sake Story   *20*

The Beginning   20 / The Turmoil   22 / The Rise and
Fall   25 / The Revolution   26 / Yamaguchi Terroir: Is There
or Isn't There?   28

The Sake Breweries and Their Communities

Eastern Yamaguchi   *34*

Iwakuni

1. Asahi Shuzo   36
2. Horie Sakaba   44
3. Murashige Shuzo   50
4. Sakai Shuzo   56
5. Yaoshin Shuzo   62

   CONNECTIONS: YAMAGUCHI AND SAKE RICE   68

Eastern / Central Yamaguchi   *74*

Shunan

6. Hatsumomidi   76
7. Nakashimaya Shuzojo   82
8. Yamagata Honten   89

   CONNECTIONS: SAKE SHOPS AND BARS   96

Kudamatsu

9. Kinfundo Shuzo   100

Central Yamaguchi   *105*

Yamaguchi City

10. Kanemitsu Shuzo   107
11. Shintani Shuzo   112
12. Yamashiroya Shuzo   118

CONNECTIONS: DOBUROKU AND THE ROOTS OF SAKE 122

Hofu

13. Takeuchi Shuzojo 125

Western Yamaguchi 130

Shimonoseki

14. Choshu Shuzo 134
15. Shimonoseki Shuzo 140

San'yo-Onoda

16. Nagayama Shuzo 146

Mine

17. Ohmine Shuzo 152

CONNECTIONS: SAKE AND DINING 157

Ube

18. Nagayama Honke Shuzojo 160

Northern Yamaguchi 166

Abu/Hagi

19. Abu no Tsuru Shuzo 168
20. Iwasaki Shuzo 174
21. Nakamura Shuzo 180
22. Okazaki Shuzojo 185
23. Sumikawa Shuzojo 190
24. Yachiyo Shuzo 197

CONNECTIONS: CERAMIC ARTISTS 203

Travel Information

Visiting Yamaguchi 210

Getting to Yamaguchi 210 / Getting Around Yamaguchi 210 / Places of Interest for the Traveler and Sake Lover 211

Afterword 226
Acknowledgments 227

Foreword

When it comes to the world of sake, what does regionality mean, really? The concept of terroir that pervades the wine industry is centered on geology and geography–the trifecta of soil, slope, and sun that imparts unique characteristics to the grapes from a particular area. In a broader context, the term refers to "a sense of place," which encompasses ideas about how a product should be made and how it should taste.

This seems logical when you consider that wine is an agricultural product whose flavor depends largely upon the variety and condition of the grapes used. As a wine drinker, I can get an idea of what a wine will taste like based on its area of origin, confident in my knowledge that Napa Valley Cabernet Sauvignon will exhibit a vastly different flavor profile from Côte de Beaune Pinot Noir. Sake, on the other hand, presents a more complicated picture. After all, would you expect anything less from a drink that harnesses the microbial magic of a benign fungus to kick-start the complex processes of multiple-parallel fermentation? Rice used for sake brewing can be shipped all over the country, and most experts will tell you that sake's character relies more on the artistry of the toji (master brewer) than the type of rice used or where it was grown. Sake made with the same rice—even using the same yeast strain, in the same region—will taste different in the hands of different brewers.

Indeed, sake is as much about people as it is about place. The decisions made by each brewery determine the extent to which collective social memory—the local food culture, taste preferences, and traditional brewing philosophies—informs the final product. In the case of a relatively young (or, more precisely, recently reborn) sake-making region like Yamaguchi, the influence of individual personalities can be felt strongly. The prefecture is full of mavericks who are defining regional character in their own ways. In the pages of *Discovering Yamaguchi Sake: A Taster's Guide to Breweries, Culture, and Terrain,* author Jim Rion introduces the iconoclasts and out-of-the box thinkers behind the area's sake revolution—from Sakurai Hiroshi, who transformed the ailing Asahi Shuzo into one of the world's most successful producers of ultra-premium daiginjo, to Nagayama Takahiro, whose love of Burgundy wine inspired him to embrace a *domaine*-style approach to rice cultivation and sake making at Nagayama Honke Shuzojo, and Okamoto Susumu, who is writing the next chapter in the history of Choshu Shuzo with the help of female toji Fujioka Miki.

The human stories at the heart of this book paint a vivid picture of a dynamic area with an exciting future. Rion renders these narratives in the loving detail they deserve, while providing wider context for each. He explores Yamaguchi's tumultuous past and roams across its varied terrain, leading readers from the charred moonscape of the Akiyoshidai Plateau, through the terraced rice fields of Hagi, to the palm-tree-lined port of Shimonoseki. Each section highlights cultural connections that go beyond the confines of the brewery, be it the region's legacy of agriculture, the bars and restaurants where sake is served, or ceramic artists crafting exquisite vessels that enhance the dining experience. By taking a deep dive into a single production area, this volume represents an evolution in the genre of books about sake and invites us to consider regionality as a living mode of expression, rather than a fixed construct. Sake's terroir is much like the author's conception of history—a "woven cloth where every thread touches each other." In this book, Rion attempts to untangle the knots, one shimmering thread at a time.

Melinda Joe

Preface

"Sake to the flesh, haiku to the soul; sake is haiku for the flesh, haiku is sake for the soul."
—from Taneda Santoka's *Travel Journals*, September 20, 1930

The poet, monk, and wanderer Taneda Santoka was born in what is now Hofu, Yamaguchi Prefecture, in 1882. He gained fame for his "free haiku," short poems that eschewed traditional formal haiku style in favor of direct expression. He often used themes of mountains and water in his work, reflecting, perhaps, his almost ceaseless walking through the mountains of western Japan and the cool mountain water that was often his only pleasure on those walks. Another common topic in his poetry and his journals was sake—he was, to put it bluntly, a lush. His family in fact owned a sake brewery in Hofu, although it closed only two years after it opened due to chronic mismanagement (the license passed to Kanemitsu Shuzo of Yamaguchi City, which now brews under the Santoka label; see p. 107).

Santoka would surely be pleased to know that the land of his birth, where he tried and failed to brew what he loved (too much), has become known as one of Japan's newest sake regions. Nectar born of mountain water and locally grown rice now flows from Yamaguchi to the entire world.

It is a wonder how Yamaguchi got here. Japan has roughly 1,200 sake breweries, but only 23 are found within its borders. And yet, of the nation's forty-seven prefectures, Yamaguchi was the only one to brew and ship more sake, year on year, every year for the twelve years leading up to 2020. It went from fortieth place for annual sake shipped in the 1970s—almost dead last, given that Okinawa and southern Kyushu produced so little sake in general—to fifteenth in 2019.

This mostly rural prefecture was a virtual unknown to the sake world some twenty years ago, and now it is home to arguably the world's most famous premium sake brand and to others that are starting to make global waves. Mujaku, from the Horie Sakaba brewery in Iwakuni, apparently impressed pop star Rihanna enough to convince her to stock up on a few $6,000 bottles in Dubai. Pharrell Williams and designer NIGO collaborated with Yamaguchi maverick Ohmine Shuzo—a brewery that had been mothballed until 2010—to create the new sake brand Storm Cowboy.

As even the smallest of Yamaguchi's breweries now win highest honors at awards shows all over the world, drinkers across Japan, and increasingly overseas, are finally beginning to see the name Yamaguchi on sake labels as a sign of something special, made with skill from the best ingredients. In March of 2021, Japan's government recognized that distinction for the neighboring towns of Hagi and Abu on the northern coast with a Geographical Indication, GI Hagi, based largely on the six regional breweries' dedication to bringing the flavors of local rice and water to their sake.

I have seen this change happen, coming to Yamaguchi as I did in 2004. I watched Asahi Shuzo's label Dassai explode onto the global stage. I watched Taka become a favorite with natural wine drinkers. I watched tiny Shintani Shuzo, a brewery staffed by only three people and with nearly the smallest sake production in Japan, win platinum at Paris's Kuramaster awards. I watched as Yamaguchi became a place where sake breweries could reopen and prosper, not just falter and close.

How did Yamaguchi do this, going from total obscurity to an increasingly global name, with new breweries, new labels, and new appreciation? The answer is, like all of sake, a complex story of land, history, culture, and skill. The story of Yamaguchi sake is that of Japan writ small, a story of rise, fall, and rebirth through reinvention. It is a story of a sake revolution.

This book is an attempt to tell that story. First I trace the roots from the natural environment to the culture that it has nurtured as I examine how history has shaped the brewing industry here in Yamaguchi. The main section of the book is all about right now. It is a snapshot of every working brewery in Yamaguchi, reflecting the community bonds that create sake and its culture. I have visited the breweries, talked to brewers and staff, drunk the water, and seen fields where Yamaguchi Yamada Nishiki rice is grown. I have tasted the sake, too, and by asking the breweries (when they were willing) to single out one of their products to introduce in this book, I hope to show how a single bottle of sake can express and encapsulate a time, a place, and a story—as well as hold a delicious drink. Finally, to the curious sake drinker who comes to Yamaguchi Prefecture in search of the sake, I offer a small travel guide with a bit of tourist information and recommendations on places to sample local brews.

So, come on, let's go way off the beaten track and see what this newborn sake region of Yamaguchi has to offer! Pour a cup, think of the mountains, and drink deep!

NOTE ON NAMES AND LISTINGS

In this book, Japanese personal names follow the Japanese order. For any individual, the FAMILY NAME comes first, then the GIVEN NAME: *Suzuki Taro is a member of the Suzuki family*. Subsequent references to individuals in the same chapter will use the family name: *Suzuki is a sake brewer.* If multiple family members are mentioned in the same text section, the given name may be used: *Suzuki Yumi is Taro's sister. Yumi is now the toji at their brewery.*

Macrons, the bars over letters to indicate longer Japanese vowel sounds, especially for *o* and *u*, have been omitted since brewers and brewery labels use them inconsistently for domestic and export purposes. You needn't worry that your pronunciation will be misunderstood.

Brewery listings include website addresses; many websites are in Japanese only or have only brief sections in English or other languages.

Prices, label descriptions, admissions fees, opening hours, and other information related to travel and visiting brewers are current as of the date of publication and are subject to change. Please check details before you go.

Sake Terms and Classifications

The following Japanese words are used in the discussions about sake and sake brewing in this book. For more detailed information on the process of sake making, check out the article "How Sake Is Made" at https://en.sake-times.com/learn/sake-101-how-is-sake-made or follow the Instagram account @discoversake at https://www.instagram.com/discoversake/.

aruten: Literally, "alcohol added"; a shorthand term for any sake that has distilled alcohol added during the brewing process. The reason for adding alcohol ranges from a simple desire to increase yields in the very cheapest sake to a way to subtly adjust and enhance aromas and flavors at the absolute highest levels of competition-grade sake.

genshu: An undiluted sake. At the end of fermentation, the sake produced can reach as high as 20% ABV (higher levels are possible but must be less than 22% to be legally classified as sake), which is considered too strong for casual mealtime drinking. To reduce the ABV, sake is often diluted after pressing. *Genshu* is bottled as-is, undiluted, but in recent years breweries have been producing *genshu* in the same 15–17% ABV range as diluted sake.

kimoto: A type of fermentation starter or seed mash, called *shubo* or *moto*, perfected in the Edo period (1603–1867). Traditional *kimoto* often (but not always) involves crushing rice to a paste with wooden rods—a practice called *yamaoroshi*—and then allowing naturally occurring lactic acid bacteria to flourish. This creates an acidic environment that protects the mash from harmful bacteria. It also creates a flavorful, robust, but often quite elegant sake. The style is usually listed on labels as 生酛, 生もと, or きもとand indicates an unusual, and probably delicious, sake with complexity and depth, with occasional distinct acidity.

koji: Rice that has been inoculated with the mold *Aspergillus oryzae*. This mold digests the starch in rice to create sugar for fermentation, making sake brewing possible in a process called "multiple-parallel fermentation," where rice starch is converted to sugar at the same time that yeast converts sugar into alcohol. *Koji* also creates a variety of flavor components as it works and is considered a foundational element of sake flavor.

koku: A traditional measure of volume for rice, also used to describe sake-brewing volume. It is equal to roughly 180 liters (around 47.5 gallons) and is part of the same measurement system as the *go* (180ml), *sho* (1.8 liters), and *to* (18 liters) units used elsewhere in sake brewing.

koshu: Aged sake. There is no standard duration of aging to qualify for the term *koshu*, but most breweries call sake one to three years old *jukuseishu* (matured sake), while anything older will be *koshu*.

kura: Literally meaning something like "storehouse"; a commonly used short form of *sakagura*, meaning "sake brewery."

kuramoto: In general terms, the sake brewery as a company, but in particular the individual who owns and manages the business. In many cases, this person is a member of a family that has owned the business for generations.

kyokai kobo: Commonly called "association yeast" in English. The Brewing Society of Japan, or Nihon Jozo Kyokai, is a research and education organization dedicated to better sake brewing. It does lots of valuable work, but its most prominent job these days is supplying stable, standard yeast varieties to sake breweries. They are usually identified by a number; popular varieties include #9 and #1801.

moromi: The fermentation mash. This is usually built in three stages after the *moto* (see below) is completed. Each stage includes an addition of rice, *koji*, and water in increasing amounts.

moto: Also known as *shubo*, the starter mash that breweries make to allow yeast cells to multiply to a sustainable level before building the main fermentation mash. Proper *moto* making allows the microorganisms that make sake (yeast, *koji* mold, and various bacteria) to reach stability so they are not overwhelmed when rice is added in building the full fermentation mash or *moromi.*

muroka: Unfiltered. After the fermentation is finished, sake must legally have the solids removed from the liquid in a process that I refer to in this book as "pressing." After pressing, the sake is stored in tanks and then (often) run through another filtration process to clarify the sake and remove any residual solids, called *roka* in Japanese. Filtration processes can vary drastically and sometimes use activated charcoal. In recent years, breweries are releasing more unfiltered sake.

namazake (or just ***nama***): Unpasteurized sake. Sake is typically pasteurized twice after pressing: once immediately and again at bottling. *Namazake*, however, is not pasteurized at all. Some types of *namazake* are only pasteurized once; *namachozo* is only pasteurized on bottling, and *namazume* is only pasteurized immediately after pressing.

National Research Institute of Brewing (NRIB): A governmental organization dedicated to research and development in the liquor production field. The NRIB offers training and supplies for sake brewers.

sakagura: Literally, "liquor storehouse"; a common term for sake breweries in general as well as other traditional producers of alcoholic beverages. Commonly shortened to *kura.*

sake meter value (SMV): A measure of residual sugar in a brew, in which a negative value indicates more sugar, and positive values less. Higher is drier.

seimaibuai: The percentage of a rice grain that remains after milling, sometimes called the polishing or milling ratio. For example, a *seimaibuai* of 60% means that 40% of the rice has been milled away and 60% is left. The goal of milling is to reduce the amounts of fats and proteins—concentrated in the outer layers of the rice grains—that many people believe result in off-flavors.

shuzo: Literally, "alcohol maker," a common part of breweries' names. The term is also used by spirit distilleries.

sokujomoto: The modern "quick" fermentation starter method, in which the lactic fermentation of *kimoto* and *yamahai moto* is replaced by simply pouring lactic acid into the starter. Some 90% of all sake brewed today uses this starter method.

toji: The head of brewing, a role that includes not only the craft of brewing but also production planning (rice purchasing, personnel, etc.) and management of the brewing staff.

yamahai: A type of *moto*, the starter mash that breweries make to allow yeast cells to multiply to a sustainable level before building the main fermentation mash. The full name is *yamaoroshi haishi*, meaning "an end to *yamaoroshi*" (see the entry for *kimoto*). This technique was developed from the *kimoto* method around 1910 and uses warm water and temperature control to encourage natural dissolution of the rice in order to promote lactic acid bacteria to grow and create an acidic environment suitable for yeast. It was very quickly replaced by a modern quick starter, which uses chemical reactions and laboratory-made lactic acid for much faster *moto* building. *Yamahai* appears on labels as 山廃 or やまはい. It often indicates a very robust, sometimes sour or lactic sake.

About Sake Classification

What is now commonly called sake in English, the fermented beverage made from rice, rice *koji*, and yeast, is legally identified as *seishu* (refined alcohol) or commonly *nihonshu* (Japanese alcohol) in Japan. Types of sake are organized into a few different classes that are important to know about.

TOKUTEIMEISHOSHU (SPECIAL DESIGNATION SAKE)

The following classifications are legally defined in Japan, and their use on labels is allowed based on certain minimum brewing-process requirements. One condition shared by all is that the rice used must be graded and certified by a government inspector, although that rice does not have to be a recognized brewing rice.

junmai: This sake cannot contain any ingredients apart from rice, rice *koji*, yeast, and water. You will often see this word used in conjunction with other classifications below and sometimes with the term *tokubetsu* (special) that indicates some kind of unusual feature of the brewing process. There is no standard requirement for *tokubetsu*, so the actual indication often remains vague; it could be that the rice used was special or the milling ratio reached *ginjo* levels.

ginjo: A class of sake made from rice that has been milled to 60% or less and brewed in a particularly careful process known as *ginjo-zukuri*. The details of this process can vary widely, but one common feature is that fermentation happens slowly at very low temperatures to bring out aromatic elements.

daiginjo: A class of sake made from rice that has been milled to 50% or less and brewed in an even more delicate version of the *ginjo-zukuri* process. This was once very difficult to achieve, so the common attitude is that *daiginjo* brewing represents the

"peak" of the sake-brewing art. However, this attitude is changing as *daiginjo* becomes more commonplace.

honjozo: A class of sake made from rice that has been milled to
70% or less and includes an addition of distilled alcohol late in
the fermentation process. This addition can help stabilize the
sake, lighten flavor, and enhance certain aroma elements that
are alcohol soluble. The amount of alcohol cannot exceed 10% by
weight of the rice used in fermentation.

EVERYTHING ELSE

Legally defined *seishu* that fails to meet even one of the requirements of the special designation sake above is commonly called
futsushu or *ippanshu*, which really only means "normal sake." This
diverse group is still by far the market leader in Japan and represents the real heart of regionality and local flavor. Brewers tend
to make it from cheaper rice that may or may not be graded by a
government certifier, and it can contain other additives to increase
yields, which helps keep prices reasonable. It almost always has
added distilled alcohol like *honjozo*, both to adjust flavor and stability and to boost volume, but the maximum limit is higher. It can
also include added sweeteners, amino acid flavorings, or organic
acid stabilizing agents. The total additives cannot exceed 50% by
weight of the rice used. In practical terms, this means that the
brewery is legally allowed to double the sake yield using these additives. However, many smaller sake breweries show restraint here
due to quality and taste concerns. The best *futsushu* will have no
more than three ingredients on the label: rice, rice *koji*, and (usually
but not always) distilled alcohol.

gave way to the more agricultural Yayoi culture around 300 BCE with the coming of wet-field rice cultivation from the Asian mainland. With the increase in rice, of course, came an excess that could be fermented into a drink: the roots of sake.

People have fermented alcohol from rice in Japan ever since the grain become widely cultivated here—first in the wide plains of Kyushu to the south, then up through Yamaguchi all the way across the main island. In Yamaguchi, wet-field, or paddy, farming was initially clustered on the fertile, relatively flat Abu highlands on the northern coast and the wider fields of the Suo Plain to the southeast. These areas, dominated by the city of Hagi in the north and Iwakuni to the south, are still centers for sake brewing because, at its heart, sake is rice, and they are where the rice grows best.

Despite its uneven terrain, Yamaguchi is well gifted with farms. Rains falling on the mountains filter through green forest, rich soil, and bedrock to feed countless springs and rivers that have carved valleys and caves all through the prefecture. That water nourishes a patchwork of rice paddies (as well as supplying breweries with another vital resource) that now cover about half of Yamaguchi's arable land. Rice had become the backbone of the area's economy long before Japan, as a nation, existed, but it was with the Edo period, starting in 1603, that its production really exploded.

History can often read like a series of events, but it is more like a web, a woven cloth where every thread touches another. How else can we understand why the decisive Battle of Sekigahara of 1600 CE, where Tokugawa Ieyasu defeated his Toyotomi clan rivals half a nation away, helped expand Yamaguchi's sake brewing to unprecedented heights in the nineteenth century? For Ieyasu won that battle—which paved the way for him to become Japan's supreme ruler, or shogun—largely because Mori Terumoto's western armies, manned in part by the people of what is now Yamaguchi, failed to show up and support their allies—a betrayal orchestrated by

Mori retainer Kikkawa Hiroie, lord of Iwakuni Castle. Tokugawa rewarded the betrayal by allowing Mori to live, but he stripped him of most of his western lands except the two provinces of Nagato no Kuni and Suo no Kuni, which we now know as Yamaguchi.

Mori moved his capital to Hagi and built a castle there around 1608. To cut costs, he retired many of his samurai retainers and gave them undeveloped farmland for building rice paddies that would expand agricultural income. Rice cultivation steadily increased, and with it local sake brewing. Excess rice, when it was available, was turned into sake in every village in both provinces, with larger towns having up to ten breweries supplying peasant and lord alike. Records from the time are sparse, but in the mid-1700s there appear to have been some two hundred officially recognized sake producers. Of course, there were likely many more unofficial ones producing thick, rough *doburoku* (unfiltered, unrefined sake) in the hills and valleys. Today, four of Yamaguchi's twenty-three sake breweries can trace their history back to the Edo period.

The Turmoil

The Mori clan and their former samurai never forgot their humiliating fall. Resentment at the shogun's treatment festered and grew for two long centuries, until it culminated in full-on rebellion. In the 1860s, the sons of notable samurai families and even the Mori lord conspired to form the Satsuma Alliance with powerful clans from the island of Kyushu, just to the south of Yamaguchi. Together, they eventually defeated the shogun's armies to restore the emperor to supreme political power and end the military rule that had lasted throughout the Edo period.

This was the Meiji Restoration, or Meiji Ishin, of 1868, which thrust Japan into the modern age under a democratic administration serving the emperor. Powerful Yamaguchi families were right at the center. The new government, led by Yamaguchi-born Prime Minister Ito Hirobumi, reorganized the old feudal domains into prefectures and set Japan on its race into modernity. The two domains of Suo and Nagato were merged into Yamaguchi Prefecture, and the capital officially settled in Yamaguchi City. And, of course, sake was there through all these changes. The new government relaxed brewing license controls, creating a huge spike in sanctioned brewers. Historians estimate the peak number just after the Meiji Restoration at around a thousand breweries making Yamaguchi sake. Over half of the Yamaguchi breweries still operating today were founded during the Meiji period (1868–1912), and seven of those appeared within its first twenty years.

The number of breweries has dwindled ever since, though. The early years of Meiji saw a sudden drop as oversaturation of the market meant that many of the new upstarts disappeared as quickly as they appeared.

Those first few years after the Meiji Restoration were tumultuous ones for the nation as a whole, of course. The economy changed as an industrial base was added to the traditional agricultural one. The large ports along the gentle Seto Inland Sea eventually became centers for industrial shipping and then factory sites themselves as rail lines spread the length of Japan. Yamaguchi became a center for shipbuilding, chemical manufacturing, heavy machinery, and metal working, industries that still form a core part of the local economy. Agriculture was concentrated in the central and northern parts of the prefecture, away from the heavily developed San'yo coast.

Sake brewing has always been adjacent to agricultural work, and in fact most winter sake brewers were farmers in the warm seasons. When seasonal agriculture was replaced by year-round industrial work, sake breweries began to struggle to find brewing staff. Yamaguchi's industrialization accelerated the closing of sake brewers in a trend that would continue to the present day, but with the coming

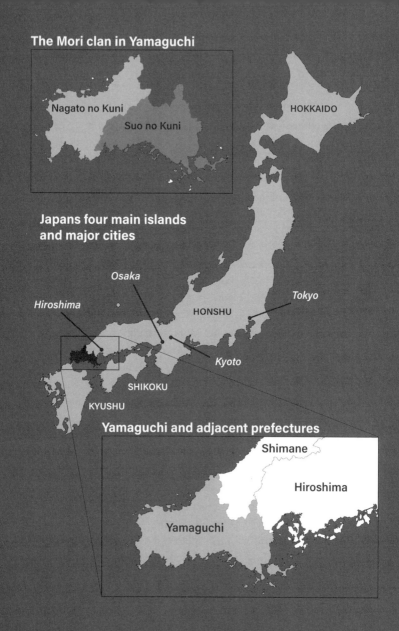

The Mori clan in Yamaguchi

Nagato no Kuni

Suo no Kuni

Japans four main islands and major cities

Hiroshima

Osaka

Tokyo

HONSHU

HOKKAIDO

Kyoto

SHIKOKU

KYUSHU

Yamaguchi and adjacent prefectures

Shimane

Hiroshima

Yamaguchi

of the Showa era (1926–89) and its terrible war, the losses became enormous.

War preparations kicked industrialization into high gear, and many brewers were drafted—not only as soldiers but as brewers for Japan's overseas colonies and bases. The heavily industrialized San'yo coast was eventually a prime target for bombing runs, which naturally took a toll on the surrounding communities and their sake breweries. From the post–Meiji Restoration peak of a thousand breweries, the number had fallen to about three hundred by the end of the war.

The Rise and Fall

After the war, though, the story changed. The nation of Japan rushed into postwar rebuilding and created an economic boom. The people who drove that boom were sake drinkers. The sake market grew, and grew, and grew for almost three decades, and early on the major brands realized they could not keep up with demand. Regulations on rice purchasing and constraints on construction forced them to get creative in filling their bottles, and so was born *okeuri*: tank sales or, in other words, contracted production. The big brands wrote out recipes for the sake they needed, contracted smaller, regional breweries to make it, and bought it by the tank. The resulting deal was tax-free to the actual maker, as all the tax burden was assumed by the contractor.

The practice supported small breweries all over Japan, but Yamaguchi seems to have thrown itself into *okeuri* with particular gusto. Many small Yamaguchi breweries were selling the bulk of their production to labels in other prefectures—Hiroshima, Hyogo, and Kyoto. It was a source of guaranteed, tax-free sales, but there was a hidden price.

Smaller breweries began to focus so much on their guaranteed customers further afield that they often ignored local ones. In 1973, Yamaguchi was producing around 140,000 koku (roughly 25.2 million liters, or 6.7 million gallons) of sake, almost all of it headed outside of the prefecture. Some even went so far as to advertise the national brands where their sake ended up, rather than their own labels. Drinkers responded in kind by increasingly preferring those major brands, and Yamaguchi lost much of its local sake market. That loss would soon be felt.

The oil crisis of 1973 killed the cash cow. The sake market plummeted as people curtailed spending, and at the same time eases in government rice-purchasing regulations meant that the major sake producers suddenly had no problem filling demand. The made-to-order contracts ended, and many small breweries were forced to realize they had no other market to turn to.

It was a slaughter. Breweries struggled to stay afloat but closed one after another. In 1984, there were still 99 left. Now, in 2022, there are only 23 producing breweries. How did they survive?

The Revolution

Yamaguchi sake survived through reinvention. In the 1980s, Japan began to experience what people now call the "*jizake* boom." *Jizake* is a catch-all term for sake produced by smaller brewers for local markets, as opposed to the major players like Hakutsuru or Gekkeikan that supply the whole world. In the 1980s, urban drinkers realized the countryside was full of hidden gems selling higher quality sake at lower prices, and sake retailers began scouring distant regions to supply just that. Yamaguchi, however, was missing out. So many of its breweries had spent all their time making cheap sake to order that there were very few left with the skills or the financial base to make the quality sake that the booming urban market wanted.

Some people, like brewery Asahi Shuzo's former president Sakurai Hiroshi, saw what had to be done. Sakurai took over his family brewery in the late 1980s, only to see that it was soon headed for bankruptcy. His response saved the brewery and set it on a course to international stardom: make only premium sake, and target people everywhere. The result was Dassai, now considered one of the world's great sake brands. He was not alone, of course, nor was he even the first. Yamagata Honten, Nagayama Shuzo, and Sumikawa Shuzo all started releasing premium sake—particularly the new junmai, so-called "pure-rice" sake, expressions—in the 1980s. The trail they blazed guided all the rest into a new future.

Yamagata Toshiro, Yamagata Honten's kuramoto (owner/president), was particularly influential in helping Yamaguchi brewers as a group cooperate in redefining what Yamaguchi sake could be. He spearheaded a project called Yamaguchi Jizake Ishin—the Yamaguchi Local Sake Revolution. Through the Yamaguchi Sake Brewers Association, which Yamagata headed from 2016 to 2022, the member breweries could share skills, cooperate in marketing events in the major urban centers, and work together to create a new image of high quality and local sourcing for Yamaguchi sake.

As they began to succeed, with Dassai in particular becoming a shining star in the premium-sake heavens, local government and agricultural organizations joined in. Making premium sake requires premium-sake rice, and despite Yamaguchi's agricultural prowess, the particular strains of rice that sake brewers value—Yamada Nishiki, Gohyakumangoku, Omachi, etc.—were all coming from outside the prefecture. The relevant authorities began working with current sources of sake-rice seed and even started breeding a new strain of Yamaguchi-only sake rice. The results have been pretty surprising: In roughly a decade, Yamaguchi went from producing zero Yamada Nishiki to becoming the third-largest growing region in Japan (even so, it is still very far behind the leader, Hyogo Prefecture).

Yamaguchi's own sake rice—Saito no Shizuku—is now being used by breweries all over the prefecture to make award-winning sake.

Every sake brewery in Yamaguchi now uses some percentage of Yamaguchi-grown rice, and some are able to source a hundred percent of their needs within the prefecture. Breweries around Hagi have gone so far as to team up with local rice farmers to grow, polish, and brew their rice totally within the Hagi area, which has helped earn them their own Geographical Indication, recognizing the intense focus on local sourcing and local style. Locality has become a major goal of all the smaller breweries in Yamaguchi. Call it terroir, call it regionality, call it a return to roots, but Yamaguchi sake is increasingly rooted directly in the soil around the brewery and bound by ties of community that give the sake a value far beyond the price on the bottle.

Yamaguchi Terroir: Is There or Isn't There?

Terroir. It has become the talking point of the drinks world, be it wine or whisky, and sake is no exception. I must admit that, read as I can and ask who I will, I have yet to establish a clear idea of what the term actually means.

Is terroir a physical thing, a flavor expressing the nature of the soil and climate—as the word itself would seem to hint—in a finished product? One that experienced people can identify purely from tasting the sake?

Or is terroir a philosophical and cultural expression of the brewer's community and the way it guides their decisions in the brewery?

If it is the former, a physical thing, I see very little room for terroir to be meaningful in sake. Sake is such a purely process-built drink, distanced from the soil through milling, intentional physical changes in the brewery, and post-brewing process choices, that the influences of soil and sun are tenuous at best.

Even the basic concept of regionality in sake is defined in only the most general way. As sake evangelist John Gauntner puts it, as you move from east to west (which, for Japan, also means north to south) sake generally starts out as a crisp, light, dry drink (i.e., the *tanrei karakuchi* style of Niigata) and then becomes a richer, more full-bodied one. While you may not be able to drink a single sake and say, "Ah, this is a Saga sake," if you compare a Niigata sake and a Fukuoka one you will usually be able to tell which is which on the first sip. Emphasis on the "usually." Beyond that, even the most educated palate will be challenged to identify specific areas.

But if terroir refers to the latter idea, a philosophical and cultural narrative woven by the brewer, the farmers, and local culture, then yes—of course there is terroir in sake. Sake is a product of its time and place and expresses ideas about its source in its own way. Yamaguchi sake is a sake of western Japan, and it follows the trend of richer and sweeter sake because of the influences of climate, diet, and history that run throughout the region. At the same time, each brewery in Yamaguchi makes sake its own way. Many brewers are strict about using locally sourced rice in their sake as well, to express their commitment to the farming communities around them. They make sake to match the tastes of customers both local and further afield, but their own tastes and experiences guide their hands in ways conscious and unconscious. Sake brewing is a balance of individual tastes and the unseen influences that create them.

These influences are not even uniform within the current place we call "Yamaguchi." Long before the area was defined by the national government, it was defined by physical elements of mountain, highland, plain and coast. The old borders of the Nagato no Kuni and Suo no Kuni domains were carved by nature before they were codified into law. Nature also influenced the foodways of the people living there, which in turn guided the sake and the people who made it, and still do.

One key to understanding the sake-making culture in Yamaguchi is the toji guilds. Toji is the title given to the chief brewer in a sakagura (sake brewery) who is in charge of planning production, monitoring the fermentation, and managing the workers and all the other daily processes of making sake. Toji in other words, are the keystones in sake brewing. Traditionally, these highly skilled brewers were hired and trained through a guild system. The two Yamaguchi guilds began centuries ago and so correspond to the old provinces: Otsu Toji were the northern Nagato brewers, while Kumage Toji were the southern Suo brewers.

Prior to World War II, the Kumage Toji guild was the larger of the two and was also the sixth largest in Japan. Records from 1935 say it included 500 toji and 2,800 kurabito (the general brewing staff). The Otsu Toji guild in the northern region was smaller, but still served a population spreading from Fukuoka to Shimane. The regions they served influenced the sake they brewed.

The Otsu Toji brewed for people eating cuisine based on seafood from the open seas and flavored with sweet, full-bodied soy sauce. This guided the sake there toward rich and sweet expressions, or *nojun amakuchi* in Japanese. These brews have a relatively full breadth of amino acids to give depth beyond simple sweetness. Reflecting the region's history of inward-turned isolation, the Otsu Toji were brewing for small, tightknit communities centered around the old capital of Hagi and tended to resist outside influence.

The Kumage Toji were a more widespread group that sent brewers to Kyushu, Hiroshima, and even overseas to Japanese colonies. Thus, their style came under the influence of a number of external trends. The Kumage Toji developed a looser range of brewing styles to create a wider variety of sake, although the western-Japan trend toward full-bodied, *nojun* sake was still the theme around which those variations were woven.

These two guilds still exist, although greatly diminished in size. No one wants to discuss guild secrets in detail, but everyone agrees that only a handful of members of either are left. Many of Yamaguchi's modern brewers studied at university and then learned on the job at breweries elsewhere rather than through the traditional guild system, but some are still guild members. Former toji Nakama Fumihiko of Sakai Shuzo (known for its brand Gokyo) is the current head of the Otsu Toji, for example, and Iwasaki Kiichiro of Iwasaki Shuzo (Choyo Fukumusume) trained under both an Otsu and Kumage toji at his family brewery.

The sake brewed in Yamaguchi today, then, exists as part of a long cultural history that has been shaped by food culture, which itself was shaped by environment. Nothing happens in a vacuum, and the threads of nature and culture weave through the sake of Yamaguchi now just as surely as they did four hundred years ago.

If you want to call that terroir, then I embrace its role in sake. Yes, explore the ephemeral terroir of sake. Learn the history, learn the culture, learn the heart that makes sake what it is, and with every bottle you open or sip you take, deepen your own connection to the people who bring these divine droplets to your palate.

Now, let's meet those people.

The Sake Breweries and Their Communities

Eastern Yamaguchi
Iwakuni 36

IWAKUNI (population 129,091 as of 2022) stands at the mouth of Yamaguchi's largest river, the Nishiki, where it flows into the Seto Inland Sea. Iwakuni was the Edo-period domain capital of the Kikkawa lords, who ruled from a castle atop Mt. Yokoyama (sometimes locally called Mt. Shiroyama—Castle Mountain). The Kikkawa were retainers to the Mori clan, and Kikkawa Hiroie (1561–1626) was behind the plan that kept Mori Terumoto from leading the western armies to aid the Toyotomi at the Battle of Sekigahara, directly contributing to Tokugawa Ieyasu's victory but also leading to the Mori's fall in stature.

The Kikkawa family built Kintai Bridge, or Kintai-kyo, across the Nishiki River in 1673, and its five graceful wooden arches remain a symbol of the town and its history, although the bridge itself has been rebuilt a number of times. The wealthy clan's contributions to local culture have also been preserved in part in Kikko Park, a complex of museums, tree-lined plazas, and shops at the foot of Mt. Yokoyama. White-walled samurai manor houses remain around its perimeter, some of which still serve as private homes.

On paper, Iwakuni has five sake breweries, but two of them are quite far from the city center, in tiny villages that are only nominally part of the city. Asahi Shuzo, makers of Yamaguchi's most famous brand Dassai, is found in a distant mountain valley beside a tributary stream for the Nishiki. In another distant mountain valley is Horie Sakaba, makers of Kinsuzume. Still, Iwakuni is proud of its sake, and you will be able to find all of the local labels at restaurants, convenience stores, and souvenir shops throughout the city. For more information on visiting Iwakuni, see "Places of Interest for the Traveler and Sake Lover" at the end of this book.

Iwakuni sake is universally of high quality, if surprisingly varied. One important development in the city's brewing came when Miura Senzaburo revealed his soft-water brewing technique in 1887. Miura was working in Hiroshima, where the water was much softer than that of famous brewing centers like Nada (Hyogo Prefecture) or Fushimi in Kyoto, and he had a hard time brewing successfully because of it. After he developed a technique to brew excellent sake using this soft water, Hiroshima became one of the nation's biggest brewing centers. Iwakuni is physically near Hiroshima, and the Nishiki River flowing through it similarly supplies extremely soft brewing water. Brewers in central Iwakuni were thus quickly influenced by the refined Hiroshima style of brewing, which delivered sake worlds apart from the richer-flavored sake in the rest of Yamaguchi. Gokyo and Gangi are particularly good examples of this, while outlying Horie Sakaba's Kinsuzume sake is made with harder water and demonstrates an interesting counterpoint.

Asahi Shuzo
旭酒造

Founded 1948

Kuramoto	Sakurai Kazuhiro
Toji	none
Production	35,000 koku / 6.3 million liters
Main Label(s)	Dassai 獺祭
Export Label(s)	Dassai
Homepage	https://www.asahishuzo.ne.jp/en/
Tours	available with reservations; offers English, French, and Chinese support

There is something shocking about visiting Asahi Shuzo. The slogan they used until 2021, "a little sake brewery deep in the mountains," was absurdly inappropriate. Yes, its home in the tiny community of Shuto is deep in the mountains, but for the last few years, no meaning of the word "small" could apply.

Found about a thirty-five-minute drive from central Iwakuni, Shuto is a cluster of houses strung along a mountain stream feeding the Nishiki River. It is only accessible via a winding two-lane mountain road off Highway 2, and as you wend your way uphill Asahi makes its presence known early. Not long after turning off the highway, you see two large warehouse-style buildings in white and brown displaying the Dassai logo painted several meters high. Each building is itself larger than most of the sake breweries in Yamaguchi, but this is just the shipping and rice-polishing facility—the actual brewery is still over a kilometer away.

As you drive into town, the road curves around a mountain slope to reveal something totally unexpected: On the right is a low wooden building made of unevenly but deliberately spaced wooden slats connected by a uniquely abstract wooden bridge to a twelve-story block of steel completely dominating the surroundings. This, finally, is Asahi Shuzo proper, perhaps the largest producer of jun-mai daiginjo sake in the world. The low building is the brewery-run shop, designed by famed Japanese architect Kengo Kuma—as was the bridge between it and the brewery tower. The landscape here is so mountainous that when the original brewery building was no longer big enough to meet production demands, the only choice was to build up, rather than out, and build up they did. The first two floors are the administration offices, floors three to ten are produc-tion, the eleventh floor holds conference facilities, and the twelfth floor is home to former president and current board chair Sakurai Hiroshi. The production area is packed with innovations—immense koji-making rooms (*muro*), which the company calls the largest in Japan (two of them!); custom-designed ventilation and koji tables; three rooms filled with one hundred small fermentation tanks each; and a cutting-edge quality assurance laboratory.

The basic design of building being higher rather than wider was later adapted by Sumikawa Shuzo, but the scale here is incomparable. Dassai makes nearly twelve times as much as the second-largest kura in Yamaguchi, Sakai Shuzo (Gokyo), and fifteen times as much as Sumikawa. It can be difficult to wrap your head around the fact that some thirty years ago Asahi Shuzo was on the verge of collapse. It was an also-ran in Yamaguchi's minor sake industry, making standard futsushu under the label Asahifuji and unable to compete with the larger locals like Gokyo. Sakurai Hiroshi took it from complete obscurity to dominance in the premiumsake world in a single generation.

Fermentation happens in relatively small three-thousand-liter tanks, which, given the production volume, is almost impossible to believe. There are three hundred of these small tanks, all individually monitored and mixed by staff. Asahi makes a very visible point of using traditional sake-brewing techniques, just writ large.

He did it through pure focus: one style of sake, junmai daiginjo, in three easy-to-understand variations. He also was among the first Yamaguchi sake brewers to pursue major markets outside of the prefecture. His son and current CEO Sakurai Kazuhiro explains: "He knew he had to compete outside of Yamaguchi because there was no room here. So, he met with sake shops and makers in the Tokyo area, and he found that they were only interested in premium sake. If he wanted to succeed, he had to start making junmai daiginjo."

It sounds simple, but it was not. This was before the premium-sake boom really took off locally, and many of the brewers of the time simply didn't know how to approach the tricky brewing process for such sake. Sakurai hung his hopes on something that was, at first, out of reach. He pushed his toji to try, with some success, but soon the older man retired.

Sakurai was left with an increasingly common choice in the sake industry: to give up or do it himself. He did it himself. He was not an experienced brewer, but he did the work. He studied, tested, and in particular began to record hard data on sake brewing—temperature changes, water ratios, rice hardness; everything that could be measured, was. This data became a core strategy for Dassai and is what guides its sake brewing to this day. The success Sakurai built is maintained through data records that correlate everything from climate of rice origins to rice-washing water temperature.

But the focus on data, and the absence of a traditional toji in the brewery, has earned Dassai a certain stigma among local sake drinkers. Once, several years ago, I mentioned at my local barbershop that I liked Dassai, and the gang of old men there all scoffed. "Dassai's made by computers," my barber said. This attitude, gruff as it might sound, is not unusual. Nonaka Yusuke, brewery sub-manager and my plant tour guide, brought it up himself. "Lots of people believe that Dassai is all made by machine, but most of the work really is done by hand. It's very important to keep that human touch in it."

When I visited the brewery, Nonaka was intent on showcasing the human element. He showed me the rice-washing and soaking room. Here the rice is first washed mechanically (a practice more common than you might think, even at smaller breweries), but the timing and soaking are manually monitored by staff to the second, with data on the rice condition—classified by growing region, climate, and harvest date—guiding the process. The koji is all made in two massive rooms with rows of tables where staff sprinkle koji spores on steamed rice, mix and knead it by hand, and monitor the temperature and moisture content through equipment built into the tables. Fermentation happens in relatively small three-thousand-liter tanks, which, given the production volume, is almost impossible to believe. There are three hundred of these small tanks, all individually monitored and mixed by staff. Asahi makes a very visible point of using traditional sake-brewing techniques, just writ large.

Still, as Asahi is a massive brewery in one of the most modern facilities in the industry, some level of mechanization is inevitable. For example, most of the rice is steamed in an automated continuous steamer, while the shubo (starter) rice is steamed in a traditional tank-style *koshiki* steamer. President Sakurai is quick to point out, though, that every element of the process was chosen with quality in mind, rather than simple scale. "Our staff use machinery and data in the pursuit of making good sake," he says. The continuous steamer, he adds, avoids putting excessive pressure on different layers of rice, as may happen with a *koshiki*, so it, too, offers some benefit over traditional techniques. The eye to quality control is always there.

Technology is used to support staff labor in other ways as well. The koji is made by hand, but instead of controlling temperature by hand-rearranging small boxes holding batches of growing koji, the finished koji is placed on boxlike wooden tables equipped with electric fans to control temperature and moisture. After it is finished, the koji is flash frozen for later use. In this way, brewing Dassai is quite clearly at an intersection of traditional manual techniques and modern automation.

Another criticism, that Dassai's brewery has valued distant markets more than the local one, has perhaps a hint of truth in it. Much of the sake's fame and success came through international connections, some of which Asahi Shuzo actively cultivates. One of the first big boosts the sake received came after then–Prime Minister Abe Shinzo offered it to President Obama, and then again when President Obama returned the favor by serving several cases at a state dinner welcoming the Yamaguchi-native prime minister at the White House. That may not have been exactly planned by Asahi, but as Abe was a Yamaguchi native, there are inevitable rumors. Considering that there are official Dassai outlets in Paris, a planned brewery in New York state, and an enormous picture in their lobby of the late French chef Joël Robuchon sipping Dassai from a wine glass, international connections are clearly valued at Asahi. Asahi Shuzo is not the only sake brewery that pursues international markets, of course, but for Yamaguchi sake drinkers the real issue might be that, for several years, it has seemed to ignore the local one.

Sakurai was left with an increasingly common choice in the sake industry: to give up or do it himself. He did it himself. He was not an experienced brewer, but he did the work. He studied, tested, and in particular began to record hard data on sake brewing—temperature changes, water ratios, rice hardness; everything that could be measured, was. This data became a core strategy for Dassai and is what guides its sake brewing to this day.

I can personally say that, from around 2014 to 2019, Dassai became hard to find on local Yamaguchi store shelves. It was once a premium drink available even at Yamaguchi's train station kiosks, but for several years it seemed easier to get in Tokyo than the place where it was made. CEO Sakurai Kazuhiro says, "I understand people have that feeling, but for us, our biggest chance to compete and succeed was in the capital. If we had only focused on the market here in Yamaguchi, we never would have gotten strong enough to succeed. Olympic athletes can never reach their best only competing close to home, you know. . . . Shuto is still our home, though. Some in the business tell us we should move to where there is better access to shipping or go closer to our markets. But we grew up here, and the people here have supported us from the beginning. Yamaguchi is still important to us."

The local ties are quite real, of course. Asahi Shuzo is the largest purchaser of Yamaguchi-grown Yamada Nishiki—as of 2021 Yamaguchi is the third-largest producer of that rice in Japan—and it has direct contracts with rice farmers throughout the prefecture, guaranteeing a fixed yearly purchase and stable income for those farmers. It also sponsors local events and is an active participant in the prefectural sake brewers association. Most importantly, Dassai's prominence has had undeniable influence on Yamaguchi's wider reputation for sake brewing. It has attracted attention from major markets, and the premium standard it has built has certainly helped improve perceptions of Yamaguchi sake throughout Japan.

Asahi is still a major driver of Yamaguchi's overall success, not only in terms of sales and income but in less tangible areas as well. As Dassai brought attention to the potential for sake to become a premium, global beverage, other Yamaguchi sake brewers were able to leverage that attention for their own sake lines. That, in turn, has led to a general sense of optimism. Yamaguchi is now a place where sake breweries can open, rather than just close, where sake has a future, not just a past.

BREWER'S CHOICE SAKE

There is really no other sake to choose except Dassai 23 when searching for the heart of Dassai sake brewing. As CEO Sakurai Kazuhiro puts it, "This is the core of the Dassai philosophy. Delicious sake with a sense of clarity and smoothness for slow sipping."

純米大吟醸

磨き二割三分

Dassai 23
Seimaibuai: 23%
Rice: Yamada Nishiki

Its focus on this kind of flavor profile has earned Dassai a reputation for reliability, with most drinkers immediately recognizing a "Dassai flavor." Sakurai himself, though, seems to feel otherwise.

"Dassai's flavor has always evolved and improved. It changes all the time, and our flavor has never stood still," he says. "The only thing that hasn't changed is our desire to make sake that we think is delicious." The subjective nature of "delicious" aside, there is no denying that Dassai 23 is the key representative of the popular conception of "Dassai flavor."

Dassai 23 is highly aromatic, with mellow notes of banana, peach, melon, and vanilla. It is the epitome of the clean Yamada Nishiki daiginjo profile, with big, full taste and no coarseness or off flavors. The initial presentation is mellow, with a touch of banana, mango, and marshmallow, which fades into a mouth-filling sweetness with low acidity. The finish lingers, slowly drawing out into a touch of slight bitterness. There is a weight to this sake that keeps one from drinking glass after glass, which seems to be the intent of the brewery's frequent mentions of "sipping," but in some ways the clean clarity it aims for stands in the way of any deeper complexity.

This is definitely a sake that benefits from chilling, and I found that when sipped from a wine glass it went well with a mellow, creamy cheese like Brie. Which, of course, is exactly the kind of sake that Asahi Shuzo wants Dassai to be.

Horie Sakaba
堀江酒場

Founded 1764

Kuramoto	Horie Yoshio
Toji	Horie Kazumasa
Production	not disclosed
Main Label(s)	Kinsuzume 金雀
Export Label(s)	Kinsuzume, Mujaku
Homepage	http://www.horiesakaba.com
Tours	not offered

Horie Sakaba is in Nishiki-cho, a small community that, while technically part of Iwakuni City, is actually a long, winding mountain drive from the city center, making the connection tenuous at best. Nishiki-cho feels very much like its own town and weaves seamlessly into the fresh green environment of the Chugoku Mountains.

And what a lovely environment it is. The mountain forests abut the roads, and streams from the top of Mt. Mizuno'o wind through the landscape. Those streams are home to endangered giant Japanese salamanders, which grow up to two meters (six feet) and sometimes wander where they should not (the town has its own salamander rescue center). The narrow high street running through the local town center is lined with shops that have somehow survived Japan's rural depopulation with grace. Not far from that shopping street, up a steep mountain road, we find Yamaguchi Prefecture's oldest surviving sake brewery: Horie Sakaba.

Horie Sakaba was founded in 1764, during the feudal Edo period

when, according to toji Horie Kazumasa, most brewing licenses were awarded to members of the elite samurai class. The implication is, of course, that Horie himself is descended from such lofty lineage. The brewery building is undated but ostensibly goes back to the same era—Kazumasa points out a wooden rack on the wall that once apparently held weapons. Now, it holds wooden stirring poles (*kai*).

Horie has become something of a local buzz maker. Up until very recently, the brewery was extremely small scale, focusing solely on production for the local market. Like many others, it was hit hard by the post-1970s sake market decline and had barely survived for years, despite its storied history and a name that many sake lovers spoke of with something like reverence.

Sometime around 2018 I began hearing that Kinsuzume, their main label, had been reborn as a premium brand. The buzz was only helped by the fact that even when Kinsuzume was released most shops did not carry it, while the ones that did tended to sell out in days. The brewery became something of a legend, which was bolstered by the release of their super-premium line—sake that are priced from ¥33,000 to ¥77,000 in ¥11,000 increments, each one aged a year longer than the last. That's roughly $300 to $500 a bottle, prices that boggle the mind when compared to other sake brands.

And then came Mujaku. Kinsuzume translates as "golden sparrow," while Mujaku is more like "dream sparrow"—and it certainly does seem like something from a dream. This sake has been released primarily for the foreign market, especially in East Asia and the Middle East, and runs from ¥88,000 to over ¥300,000 yen for a 720ml bottle—or around $850 to $2,800. Some bottles of the most expensive have sold in Dubai for over $6,000. Mujaku is one of the most valuable sake in the world and has been seen in the hands of international celebrities. And all of it comes from this small brewery, over two hundred and fifty years old, in the green mountains of Yamaguchi.

This reflects Kazumasa's focus on quality over quantity. Very few bottles of Mujaku exist because he wants to maximize the value of each individual bottle through exacting care, rather than maximizing production to increase profits.

One of Horie's guiding principles is that every sake is made for quality, rather than quantity, which helps explain such limited availability. This is also why it does not release detailed information about overall production volume—the current toji Horie Kazumasa and his father, kuramoto Horie Yoshio, want the focus to be on the individual sake. "The different kinds of sake we make here are like expressions of ideas," Kazumasa says. "Some are for mealtimes; some are to exhibit our understanding of a specific style. At its heart, though, each one is an expression of rice."

Horie uses a wide variety of sake rice in its brewing. Naturally, it uses the ubiquitous Yamada Nishiki. It also brews with Omachi, Gohyakumangoku, and Isehikari, the latter being a variety first isolated in the fields of the storied Ise Jingu shrine in Mie Prefecture and now grown extensively in fields around Iwakuni. Isehikari is the main fermentation rice used in Mujaku (the koji is Yamada Nishiki). For this particular brew, it is milled to 18% to create a super daiginjo sake that Kazumasa describes as clear, well structured, and geared specifically for aging.

Horie Sakaba also produces sake using the traditional kimoto and yamahai methods (see pp. 13 and 16), which normally result in very boldly flavored, less aromatic sake. However, Kinsuzume versions can almost overwhelm with powerful, fruit-salad aromas. "We use ambient yeast that lives on the walls of our kura," says Kazumasa. "It makes for very aromatic sake, so we can create our own unique expression of traditional styles. For kimoto and yamahai, our focus is on the process, rather than the rice, so I want to express the potential of traditional methods in skilled hands." Mujaku, the super-premium sake, is also a kimoto, which helps it stand up to the aging it was brewed for.

"My intent for Mujaku," Kazumasa continues, "is to create a sake that fits the world's idea of wine. Wine offers a premium experience and only grows more valuable with age. Mujaku is made to do that same thing. It can be aged, and over the years its quality and value increase." This reflects Kazumasa's focus on quality over quantity. Very few bottles of Mujaku exist because he wants to maximize the value of each individual bottle through exacting care, rather than maximizing production to increase profits.

"My goal for everything I brew, not just Mujaku, is to make sake that stands the test of time. Our brewery has a long tradition, and I want to honor that, but right now I would rather look to the future than the past." The future that Kazumasa sees is one where sake joins wine as a drink of luxury, served at fine restaurants and state dinners, not just at sushi shops.

Of course, we must not ignore the lower end of Horie's brewing, because despite the hefty price tags of the premium lineup, Kinsuzume is generally quite affordable. The junmai ginjo yamahai, made from Gohyakumangoku milled to 55%, is locally available for around ¥1,800 yen (roughly $15) and is, frankly, delicious. Horie even brews futsushu, though I have only seen it at the grocery store in Nishiki-cho itself and at the Kinsuzume direct sales shop. Kazumasa is intent on pushing the boundaries of the premium-sake market, but he isn't ignoring those of us who are not fabulously wealthy Dubai oil moguls or American pop stars, either. I, for one, am grateful for that.

TOJI'S CHOICE SAKE

Toji Horie Kazumasa wanted me to introduce his top premium line sake—one of the bottles that range in price from $300 to $500. I very gently explained to him that I would be more than happy to do so, but I simply couldn't afford a bottle even if one were to be found, and so he decided that Kinsuzume Hisho, their top grade of non-premium-line sake, would be acceptable.

Considering that this is a junmai daiginjo *fukurozuri* sake, which is what most breweries make only for competition submission and in many respects reflects the very pinnacle of the sake brewer's art, well, one must wonder what is going on in the even more premium brews above this line.

Most sake is pressed mechanically, using either a vertical *fune* ("boat") press or a horizontal "accordion" press, with both using physical pressure to force the liquid from the mash. However, for *fukurozuri* sake the mash is scooped into tightly woven cloth bags that are then tied shut and hung from a pole over a tank to catch the

Kinsuzume Hisho Junmai Daiginjo Tokubetsu Jozo
Seimaibuai: 40%
Rice: Yamada Nishiki

sake that drips out from gravity alone. This results in a delicacy and purity of flavor that has not known the more aggressive touch of physical pressing. It is always something special.

In the glass, this hefty sake has a clear, distinct white peach and fresh apple aroma, with mellow tones of banana, reflecting the distinct ambient yeast they use at Horie. The sake is a sweet, rich one, with a very pronounced initial mix of plum and peach, underscored by a strong note of umami. Its mouthfeel is thick and luxurious, silky smooth but delicately coating the palate.

The finish is long, slow, and luxurious. It melts into honey and vanilla notes but does not overstay and fades with fresh acidity. I found it went fantastically well with salty, semi-hard cheese like provolone and a medium cheddar, and that it goes so well with European-style accompaniments indeed reveals the toji's interest in joining the wine world.

Murashige Shuzo
村重酒造

Founded 1901 (as Morinoi Shuzo; reestablished 1951 as Murashige Shuzo)

Kuramoto	Murashige Masataka
Toji	Kaneko Keiichiro
Production	500 koku / 90 kiloliters
Main Label(s)	Kinkan Kuromatsu 金冠黒松, Murashige 村重, eight knot
Export Label(s)	Kinkan Kuromatsu, Murashige
Homepage	https://www.murashige-sake.co.jp
Tours	available with reservations; no English support on-site

Murashige Shuzo is a massive brewing complex along the Misho River, a small feeder stream for the Nishiki River in central Iwakuni, just behind the Shin-Iwakuni shinkansen station. That may sound like an urban location, but the only sight from Murashige's front door is the green slope of Mt. Yokoyama, which blocks the sun for much of the morning and keeps the brewery cooler than much of the surrounding town.

The brewery is physically one of the largest in the prefecture, comprising a few scattered concrete buildings patterned on the old white stucco and dark wood of Edo- and Meiji-period storehouses, but dating back only to the 1970s. Murashige's history is like that of the sake industry in microcosm: The original license dates back to the early Meiji period, when so many new sake breweries appeared as licensing restrictions were eased. When the original holder fell into trouble after World War II, the Murashige family took over. They found success in the postwar sake boom and moved from the shores of the

Imazu River (where Sakai Shuzo and Yaoshin Shuzo still stand) to build a massive new facility in the 1970s, when sake was at its peak.

Then, of course, came the drop in the market, and that massive facility began to see less and less use. Murashige's standard production until around 2019 was 1,000 koku / 180 kiloliters, which is at the bottom of the "mid-range" brewery size. Still, the main label Kinkan Kuromatsu has long been a mainstay for local consumers. Current fourth-generation kuramoto Murashige Masataka says, "Kinkan Kuromatsu is for serious sake drinkers. It's also the label that has the biggest competition because it's aimed at large retailers, supermarkets, and such." It is indeed one of Yamaguchi's more ubiquitous grocery store labels, alongside Gokyo.

While having a solid local fanbase for their key label might sound like a desirable foundation, a recent bump in the road has put Murashige in a precarious situation. "Our old toji was named Hinoshita. He made his own sub-label here, Hinoshita Muso, and it became a bit of a brand on its own." Hinoshita Muso was a very well-regarded Yamaguchi label, known for its modern-style smooth drinkability. In 2019, though, Hinoshita resigned. "When he quit," Masataka says, "almost all the rest of the staff did, too. Only one person from the old crew stayed on."

That meant that the brewery had to suddenly find a new toji and brewing staff, which is not so simple a task—made all the harder with the coming of the Covid-19 pandemic. "In the end, the lone remaining kurabito and I decided to manage brewing ourselves by cutting down production, and we hired some totally new staff to help out. It has not been easy."

Kuramoto Murashige, though, has taken this crisis as an opportunity. "We considered trying to maintain continuity with the Muso label, but we decided to go a completely new way to create some market differentiation." They established a new label, Murashige, for this initiative. "Most new sake labels are going the lighter, easier-drinking direction with fruity flavors and such. So, we thought why not do the exact opposite? We have a very solid core of old-fashioned sake lovers, so we could offer them something fresh." The Murashige label is now home to old-fashioned flavors, with a deep, rich, dry sake that has the heft of a futsushu in a complex, well-made junmai.

> Another new venture is focused on yeast #8, which almost completely disappeared from use for several years. This yeast produces a high level of acidity and very dry sake for the kind of drink that fell out of favor with the approach of modern junmai- and ginjo-class-focused sake brewing in the 1990s and early 2000s. Only a handful of breweries in Japan use #8 now, and Murashige claims to be one of the first to restore it to regular production.

"We just aren't sure how to express this to the public. The Kinkan Kuromatsu drinkers who have tried it actually say they prefer Murashige, but all those other people who expect something more modern aren't sure how to react," Masataka says. The man himself, though, remains optimistic. "I think we have good ideas on how to make our sake stand out. We're still getting everything together, but there are lots of plans in place."

One of those new plans is based on yeast. "I think using unusual yeasts is a clear way we can stand out. We use #9E for Murashige," the kuramoto says, amid plans to expand into other unusual yeasts. Yeast #9E is a Yamaguchi variant of the hugely popular #9 yeast and is a strong fermenter. This means that it tends to consume more sugar from the fermentation and produce a dry, deep, full-flavored sake. The yeast has been a keystone for the label, but the brewers are currently thinking about adjusting the lineup.

Another new venture is focused on yeast #8, which almost completely disappeared from use for several years. This yeast produces a high level of acidity and very dry sake for the kind of drink that fell out of favor with the approach of modern junmai- and ginjo-class-focused sake brewing in the 1990s and early 2000s. Only a handful of breweries in Japan use #8 now, and Murashige claims to be one of the first to restore it to regular production. It is exploiting the yeast's strong natural acidity to create unique expressions for a new label, eight knot, aimed at white wine drinkers and featuring crisp, dry, acidic flavors that are unusual for sake.

Kaneko Keiichiro is in charge of brewing at Murashige, though he hesitates to use the title of toji for himself. He explains: "We have two eight knot versions, Yellow (To-o) and White (Shironeri). For 2020, the first year we brewed it, White was a standard brew using #8 in a sokujo starter, and Yellow was kimoto. This year [2021], we're using kimoto for both, but White will be made with white koji instead of the usual yellow koji."

This experimental approach to new sake brewing is all the more impressive because of the small staff size and other challenges facing the brewery. "We only have five staff members, so things can be difficult. But because we've focused on small production, now we can actually handle more hand labor," Masataka says. One example: They wash all their rice by hand in small batches.

One thing that really stands out about Murashige is that, even with all of the reductions in staff and production, they are putting out an enormous variety of sake. In addition to the three discussed so far, they have a junmai brewed for sacred rituals at nearby Shirasaki Hachimangu shrine, a *kijoshu* (made using one batch of sake in place of brewing water in the fermentation process), a very unusual "fortified sake" at 30% ABV that is aged in bourbon barrels for a hybrid sake/spirit drink, and a junmai bottled in custom labels to support the nearby Hiroshima Carp professional baseball team. Some of these brews are based on blending sake from tanks that have been maturing in the Murashige warehouse for decades.

Murashige Shuzo is clearly at a crossroads, but with its clever leveraging of resources and active embrace of new ideas, and a bit of luck, the brewery is on course to recover past glory and put their beautiful facility to full use.

TOJI'S CHOICE SAKE

Kuramoto Murashige Masataka chose eight knot To-o to focus on the brewery's individuality and forward-looking plans. As one of the very few sake breweries using the near-forgotten yeast #8, Murashige seeks to create its place in the competitive sake market as a "yeast-centered" brewery.

The label eight knot is intended to appeal to wine drinkers. It uses the strong acidity and full fermentation that #8 yeast brings to create a dry, crisp sake akin to dry white wine. The Yellow version

Murashige eight knot To-o (Yellow)
Seimaibuai: 70%
Rice: Yamada Nishiki

in addition uses the traditional kimoto fermentation starter method, which results in another layer of acidity due to the action of natural lactic acid producing bacteria in the fermentation. Kimoto sake tend toward deep, firm flavors and bright acidity as well.

This particular version I sampled was clearly wine-like in presentation. The acidity looms far above what is expected of a junmai sake, but without coming across as actively sour. It brings, instead, a mouth-watering robustness to the crisp flavor, which is enticing even to someone who favors richness in their sake. It is clearly geared for mealtimes, with a focus on mouth-cleansing flavors over luxurious aromatics.

I found eight knot To-o enticing and appetizing. It certainly stands out among the typically full, rich, sweeter sake of Yamaguchi, and expressing that to drinkers looking for something different will surely result in a new group of fans.

Sakai Shuzo
酒井酒造

Founded 1871

Kuramoto	Sakai Hideki
Toji	Morishige Ken'ichi (as of October 2022)
Production	3,000 koku / 540 kiloliters a Year
Main Label(s)	Gokyo 五橋
Export Label(s)	Gokyo
Homepage	www.gokyo-sake.co.jp
Tours	available with reservations; no English support on-site.

Note: At the time of this writing, and for the twenty years previous, Sakai Shuzo's toji was Nakama Fumihiko. However, not long before publication, Nakama left Gokyo and was replaced by long-time second-in-command Morishige Ken'ichi. To preserve Nakama's legacy, we are leaving the text untouched as we wait to see how the new head brewer will influence Gokyo sake.

Sakai Shuzo stands next to the Nishiki River in Iwakuni City, not far from Iwakuni's US Marine Base. The brewery has been located here for the entirety of its one hundred fifty years, producing sake using pure, ultra-soft water from an aquifer forty meters below the riverbed. Its main label, Gokyo, is the most quintessentially "Yamaguchi" of all the sake in this book—there is not a drinker in the prefecture that does not know the brand, and not a shop that does not sell it. In an age when most Yamaguchi brewers look further and further afield for customers, the overwhelming majority of Gokyo

production is still sold within the prefecture, and the biggest seller is the Gokyo standard table-sake, or futsushu.

Which is not to say that the brewery does not offer modern, premium products. Sakai first earned national attention when its premium sake took first place at the Japan Sake Awards in 1947 (the awards do not currently name any single first-place winner); at the time, the use of ultra-soft water was a relatively recent innovation. Sakai still earns awards regularly at both the national and local level. In 2020, it earned top place in both the junmai and ginjo divisions of the Yamaguchi Sake Awards and also placed in the truncated national level competition (the National Sake Awards were suspended midway in 2020 due to the Covid-19 pandemic, so no gold prizes were awarded). The brewery went on to take gold in 2021. Sakai has also won gold at the International Wine Challenge and top awards at a variety of other domestic competitions.

Sakai Shuzo has demonstrated outstanding brewing at all levels of production, which could be what makes it a perennial Yamaguchi favorite. The brewers bring skill and focus on quality to bear on even its cheapest products, not just the most expensive. I think their futsushu is among the best I've ever had, worthy of drinking any time you're in the mood for a decent sake. When I asked about what makes it so different, toji Nakama Fumihiko explained, "It's the ingredients. We use local rice for all our sake, including the futsushu, and part of the brewer's alcohol we use is distilled from domestic rice." That comes as a surprise, as most brewers use only imported brewer's alcohol distilled from high-output materials like sugarcane. Sakai Hideki, the kuramoto, agrees: "I was a skeptic until I tried it and saw how much of a difference it makes. It's more expensive, but it really is worth it. The sake is totally different." Having drunk it, I can only concur.

"Our main concern in brewing is staying local," Sakai says. "We use only Yamaguchi-grown rice, the water is all from right here of course, and even our staff are all local." Toji Nakama himself is an Iwakuni native and has worked at Sakai essentially all his adult life. Sakai goes on, "We have an agricultural arm as well and have started to grow our own rice, but unfortunately we just don't have enough fields to supply all we need. The rest comes from direct contracts with local farmers."

In one interesting example, Sakai signed an agreement in 1996 with Toratan-mura, a group dedicated to promoting local agricultural activity, to grow brewing rice in the village of Ikachi. The farmers there grow Yamada Nishiki for Sakai Shuzo, and Sakai in turn makes premium sake from the rice for a true local win-win. Sake made with Toratan rice bears the name on the label, and Toratan premium versions have won awards for the brewery as well.

The focus on Yamaguchi is not limited to the rice and staff. Toji Nakama's personal favorite Gokyo brew is the Kiokezukuri Junmai, a sake fermented in huge cedar tanks (*kioke*). The two oldest tanks, which set the course for the brewery's expanded *kioke* brewing program some fifteen years ago, were made from trees cut in Iwakuni and turned into hand-made tanks at a workshop in Osaka.

"Everything that we are, everything that we have, comes from the local community. They are our customers, and our suppliers. We make the best we can for them, and they repay us by buying and enjoying our sake," Sakai says. When I ask him how Sakai Shuzo goes about making the best, he turns to Nakama. "He's the one who makes it, so he's the one to ask."

"Our brewing water is really soft," Nakama says, "and so everything revolves around that." This creates some challenges, in fact, as the mineral content in water is a nutrient source for the koji mold and yeast during fermentation. Low mineral content can inhibit their activity, so brewing with such soft water requires some very skillful finessing. It was this challenge that led to the development of ginjo brewing (slow, low-temperature fermentation) in Hiroshima. Thus, I have to ask about the use of traditional brewing techniques like yamahai and kimoto fermentation starters in Gokyo. These are strongly associated with the hard-water brewing of Nada, and it seems difficult to imagine these methods being used successfully with such soft water.

Gokyo's brewers first set out to make kimoto in 2004, before Nakama took over as toji. This was long before the current boom in kimoto and yamahai sake. The water from the deepest well was in fact too soft, and too pure, to make kimoto, Nakama explained. In order to successfully create these more unusual styles he had to experiment with mixing in water from other sources to find the perfect level that maintained enough minerals to sustain the natural processes but still had that Gokyo softness.

Nakama sees sake's future changing course from its current focus on delicate, highly polished daiginjo to sake that stands up well to aging—meaning richer, complex brews like kimoto and yamahai. "We have been aging sake for a long time, but we've been increasing the amount we store for the past few years. The future is in koshu," he explains.

Which is, I think, the perfect point to talk about Gokyo koshu junmai sake, as it illustrates one of the true pleasures of local sake—apocrypha. Every autumn—or almost every autumn—Sakai Shuzo bottles and releases sake that has aged for fifteen to twenty years. It is one of the highlights of my sake year, but sometimes I can't find it on the shelves. When I asked my local sake dealer why, this is what he told me—I cannot vouch for the veracity of the story, but if it's not true it should be: The Gokyo aging tanks are kept in an old mineshaft in a nearby mountain, and to bottle these tanks brewery staff have to drive up and carry small tanks by hand to their truck parked outside of the mine. There is one problem with this: bears. The mountains of Yamaguchi still have wild bears, and in years when they descend from the higher peaks in search of food, the staff can't safely get their truck loaded, and the koshu doesn't hit the market.

Thus, not only do the brewing staff have to deal with backbreaking manual labor, the vagaries of the drink market, and natural disasters ruining rice harvests, but sometimes they can't bottle their sake because of bears.

Bears!

TOJI'S CHOICE SAKE

Toji Nakama Fumihiko was quick to answer when I asked him to choose one of their sake to introduce in this book. When I asked him why he chose it, he said simply "It's my favorite. I drink it almost all the time." It is hard to argue with that!

Gokyo Junmai Kiokezukuri is a humble junmai, without any ginjo designation. However, it is fermented in very special way: in Sakai

Gokyo Junmai Kiokezukuri
Seimaibuai: 70%
Rice: koji—Yamada Nishiki;
kakemai—Isehikari

Shuzo's cedar tanks and made with the traditional kimoto starter method. Kimoto sake uses an old-fashioned process of establishing an initial fermentation base using naturally occurring lactic acid bacteria growing in the mash to create the ideal environment for robust yeast fermentation. The resulting sake usually have a pronounced acidity and deep, almost wild, flavors. The tanks themselves also act as a comforting home for the microbes that work in the mash, to help ensure a proper environment.

In Nakama's hands, none of the very unusual elements of this brew overpowers. The wood-tank fermentation offers a mild crispness and clarity, but there are no distinct cedar notes apart from a very gentle hint on the aftertaste. The kimoto acidity is clear and bright, not at all overpowering, and balances out the usual sweetness of Yamaguchi sake to prevent any lingering heaviness in the aftertaste. The umami in this sake is subtle but mouthwatering, adding to the balance of an overall compelling brew.

Kimoto junmai sake is rarely very aromatic, and this is no exception. This is a flavor sake, not an aroma one. It's a stellar meal sake for even rich meat dishes, and if you enjoy warm sake at all, I highly recommend heating it up. At around 50 degrees Celsius it really wakes up, bringing out the cedar and acid notes to actually improve the balance of an already superbly balanced junmai.

Yaoshin Shuzo
八百新酒造

Founded 1877

Kuramoto	Kobayashi Hisashige
Toji	Sakakida Yasuyuki
Production	1,400 koku / 252 kiloliters
Main Label(s)	Gangi 雁木
Export Label(s)	Gangi
Homepage	http://www.yaoshin.co.jp/en/top/
Tours	available with reservations; no English support on-site

Yaoshin Shuzo is in one of the most beautiful kura buildings in Yamaguchi. Located just a few meters from the Imazu River, which is actually a branch of the Nishiki as it flows around a delta island, it sits almost directly across the river from Sakai Shuzo (Gokyo). The front is decorated with elegant wooden posts, and the shop/tasting area is set with ornately carved decorations. The main office was once apparently a tearoom that served feudal daimyo lords traveling by riverboat to the port for trips to the capital. It is a wonderfully preserved building, and all the more impressive because for over a decade, Yaoshin focused more on beer wholesaling than sake brewing.

Like many small breweries, the post-1973 sake market collapse was hard on Yaoshin. A vicious cycle of low sales resulting in backed-up stock getting old in the warehouse, which in turn hurt the brewery's reputation, eventually led to a crisis. When current kuramoto Kobayashi Hisashige came home from school to join his

father's company, Yaoshin had two years' worth of stock in storage, and there was talk of taking a break from brewing altogether.

"But if we did that, then the toji and his crew would find other work. They wouldn't just wait around for us to start brewing again, and when we restarted there was no guarantee we would be able to bring them back," Kobayashi says. "So, my father and I decided to cut back to just one tank a year, with only the toji, Harada, and his *hashira* [the next most skilled brewing staff] doing the brewing."

During that time, the company focused its efforts on liquor and beer wholesaling, as many others did. Kobayashi, though, was unhappy with that compromise. He wanted to bring his family business back to its core of sake brewing, and his father agreed. His eventual solution was to take a chance on joining the new (at the time) junmai sake-brewing trend. He saw the focus on more premium, high-quality brewing as a way to repair the brewery's reputation and restore sales.

"It was difficult, however. The toji hadn't made junmai before, and we had trouble maintaining stable quality," Kobayashi says. The technique that finally helped solve the issue was an idea from the toji Harada. "He said that in the old days, they began their shubo starters in small tanks, called *eda-oke*, then built the first stage of the mash in the same tank. They did it because the old yeast was weaker than this new kyokai [association yeast] stuff and moving it to the bigger tank too early was a shock to the yeast."

Shubo, or fermentation starter, is usually first mixed in smaller tanks to allow healthy yeast cells to propagate in a stable environment, then moved to larger tanks to build the main fermentation in three stages (called *sandan jikomi*). Yaoshin's use of *eda-oke* keeps the moromi (the main mash) in those smaller tanks through the first stage of mash building. Initially, this allowed the junmai to reach stability and improved quality.

> That flavor identity is guided by one core belief: The ideal sake is one that is ready after pressing, with no need to rely on later processing. Most sake these days is diluted for bottling, heat treated, and run through a mechanical filter, often using activated charcoal, a step called   . These steps improve shelf life and also help the brewer adjust the flavor, aroma, and color.

The first really successful junmai brew came in 2000, and thus the Gangi label was born.

For the next few years, Yaoshin only used the *eda-oke* process for its junmai sake while still brewing some sake with added alcohol, but as they turned more of their production to junmai and ginjo classes, it eventually came to be used across the board. "I became toji in 2008, when Harada toji retired, and at that point we went 100% junmai," says Kobayashi, who passed the role to current toji

Sakakida Yasuyuki in 2021. Ever since that step to all-junmai production, a hundred percent of Gangi sake has been made using *edaoke*. The increased labor involved in transferring a larger portion of the mash mid-ferment is difficult, but Sakakida says it's worth it. "It has helped us establish a flavor identity and maintain it even as we have grown. It's hard work, but I wouldn't change it," he explains.

That flavor identity is guided by one core belief: The ideal sake is one that is ready after pressing, with no need to rely on later processing. Most sake these days is diluted for bottling, heat treated, and run through a mechanical filter, often using activated charcoal, a step called *roka*. These steps improve shelf life and also help the brewer adjust the flavor, aroma, and color. Gangi's ideal, the goal that Kobayashi had in mind when he started the label, is a sake that has no need of those adjustments and that best expresses its character as muroka nama genshu: unfiltered, unpasteurized, undiluted. Of course, the market demands some level of pasteurized sake, and at times a lower alcohol content, so Gangi does produce sake to fill those demands, but Kobayashi still views muroka nama genshu as the label's heart.

Relying on traditional techniques balanced with novelty has become a cornerstone for Yaoshin, which recently expanded its brewery and introduced a range of modern equipment to its brewing. As Sakakida says, "We want to make sure that we can express the core of Gangi sake, while still keeping up with market demands and avoiding excess pressure on staff." They maintain this delicate balance through modern data-based brewing management, using, for example, IoT-connected thermometers that transmit to smartphone apps so staff can monitor koji or moromi temperature from their homes. "Data measurement and management is essential," Kobayashi explains, "but the final decision of how to deal with the data comes down to the experience of the brewers. Human judgment always takes precedence over data."

The embrace of novelty is reflected in more than the equipment. Yaoshin Shuzo has on average one of the youngest brewing staff in Yamaguchi. Sakakida became toji at forty-eight, and most of the staff are in their twenties and thirties. These budding brewers often have their own ideas when it comes to brewing, and Kobayashi and Sakakida are careful to help nurture those initiatives. "Our sub-label Another Gangi is based around ideas that our younger brewers want to try. Obviously, we can't just do everything they come up with, but we work with them to see what's feasible, and if possible put those new products on the market. Sometimes it's only one season's worth, but if the reaction is good those ideas can become part of our regular lineup." This not only allows Yaoshin's sake to evolve and branch out, but also encourages younger people to embrace sake brewing as a career.

The brewery wants to nurture young sake drinkers, as well, to help show the versatility of this traditional beverage. "We want people to learn more about the potential for sake," Sakakida says, "that it can be a part of all kinds of events and situations." Kobayashi agrees. "Sake is the best meal drink, and not just for Japanese cuisine." At Yaoshin, the pursuit of sake that is true to its brewing character and that complements any meal guides the company as it builds on tradition to evolve into the future.

TOJI'S CHOICE SAKE

Brewers have different reasons for selecting bottles for this book's "Toji's Choice" sections. Some want to get attention for their premium lines, others just want to share their own favorite sake. Yaoshin's kuramoto Kobayashi chose Noichi for a more sentimental reason. "This was our starting point," he says.

The very first release under the Gangi label was a smooth, clean junmai muroka nama genshu, and the word "Noichi" can

要冷蔵

純米
無濾過生原酒

雁木

ノ壱

GANGI

**Gangi Noichi Junmai
Muroka Nama Genshu**
Seimaibuai: 60%
Rice: Yamada Nishiki

be translated as "the first." Kobayashi's guiding principle, he says, has always been to create sake that expresses its essential character without any post-pressing processing—or, in other words, this sake.

This unfiltered, undiluted, unpasteurized sake is initially surprising in that it does not present a lot of the up-front nama character. Noichi is a restrained, mellow junmai with a faint banana aroma. The flavor is best described as seamless. It does not stick out in any direction but simply offers a rounded, well-structured, firm sake for mealtimes. It does not overpower, it does not get overpowered, it just is.

Of all of the Gangi sake I have tried, this is clearly the best expression of the brewery's ideals and a simply delicious sake in its own right. It satisfies with a wide variety of meals and is good just for quiet sipping on its own. Really, what else does the sake drinker need?

connections

Yamaguchi and Sake Rice

Sake is rice, rice is sake. The connection between this drink and the agricultural fundament of Japan's culture cannot be overstated. Japan almost exclusively grows short-grain Japonica rice, and the variety of cultivars is mind-boggling. There are some three hundred different types of rice here, although the overwhelming majority of production is taken up by a few popular varieties. There are also a hundred and twenty varieties officially recognized as "rice well suited to brewing," or *shuzokotekimai* in Japanese. Most people just call them *sakamai*: sake rice.

New varieties of sake rice appear all the time, usually as a result of local organizations cross-breeding different varieties hoping to find one that is uniquely suited to the local climate but with all the characteristics that make it a good brewing rice. Most of these new varieties are minor players behind the undisputed king: Yamada Nishiki. Japan grows nearly twice as much Yamada Nishiki as the second-place sake rice Gohyaku-mangoku, which in turn comes in at nearly three times the volume of number three Aiyama Nishiki.

Rice that is good for brewing is markedly different from that typically found on dinner tables. Sake rice tends to have much bigger grains than table rice, and the structure of the grain is visibly different. Table rice is usually a uniform opaque white, but a close look at a grain of sake rice reveals a translucent outer layer over a white core of fluffy starch: the *shinpaku*, or white heart. This structure makes it easier for koji mold to get a big concentration of the clean starch it loves and also helps explain the emphasis on rice-polishing rates for the higher levels of premium sake. Fewer proteins and fats (found in the outer layer that is polished off) in the brewing mash means fewer off flavors (or complexity, in some opinions).

Another important factor in the rice equation is the certification process. All commodity rice in Japan, not just that for sake brewing, is priced and sold based on an official ranking system that classifies a given batch based on grain size, coloration, and the percentage of broken grains and foreign debris. Rice that fails the minimum certification is called *togai* and is sold at rock bottom prices. This is often what ends up in cheap futsushu. Above *togai* is *santo*, or third class, then *nito* (second) and, of course, *itto* (first). For sake rice there are also ranks above first class—*tokuto*, or special grade, and *tokujo*, extra-special grade. The selling price for rice of all types goes up as the ranks do, and this is reflected in the final price of the sake as well.

Yamaguchi Prefecture is full of rice fields. Just a few kilometers from the industrial centers clustered along the Seto Inland Sea, the land gives way to chains of tiny rice paddies tended by part-time and full-time farmers growing rice for food and profit. Naturally, the largest percentage is table rice, colloquially called *hanmai* in Japanese, but in recent years the amount of rice intended particularly for brewing—*shuzokotekimai* or *sakamai*—has increased dramatically.

Since around 2010, Yamaguchi's agricultural authorities and the sake brewers association have cooperated to generate a dependable local supply of sake-brewing rice in Yamaguchi, and as a result in 2020 Yamaguchi became the third-largest grower of Yamada Nishiki rice in Japan, after the overwhelming leader Hyogo Prefecture and number two Okayama. The project is still relatively new, and the numbers compared to Hyogo are quite small, but Yamaguchi's farmers are expanding production and building skill to grow rice that is at the top of the ranking charts.

Some farmers also grow popular niche varieties like Omachi or Kame no O, as well as the prefecture's own original sake rice: Saito no Shizuku, a name that can be translated as "droplets of the western capital."

Brewers do not have to use

sake rice for brewing. They can, and do, make sake from table rice, as well, sometimes to extraordinarily good result. While cheaper futsushu is commonly made from table rice, more premium styles use it as well. Omachi, the very first rice officially recognized as one well suited to brewing, started out as a common table rice and is now found in many premium or super-premium expressions. Yamaguchi has recently started experimenting with growing Omachi, although it is not an official supplier yet. The prefecture is also a center for Isehikari, another table rice that is widely considered very good for brewing; several local brewers use it in junmai and even ginjo expressions.

It is only in the last decade or so that Yamaguchi has become able to supply rice to its own breweries. The national agriculture cooperative, Japan Agriculture (JA), was once the only channel through which breweries could get the rice they needed. When Yamaguchi was not as important a sake region as it is today, JA kept its breweries lower on the priority ranks. The breweries struggled to get the good rice, so they turned to their prefectural government and the Yamaguchi brewers association for help, which in turn started putting pressure on the JA. Together the three bodies then established a system to get seed to Yamaguchi farmers and ran tests to determine whether the climate and soil could grow high-quality brewing rice. The answer, it seems, was "yes, they can."

Now, even heavy hitters like Dassai's Asahi Shuzo are buying a significant percentage of their supply from within Yamaguchi, while some smaller brewers are able to source all of their *sakamai* brewing rice from local growers. This means that local brewers can use local resources for local consumption, in a return to the true roots of sake brewing in the prefecture.

Of course, any discussion of sake rice would be incomplete without looking at where exactly the rice comes from. While in recent years some breweries have begun growing and harvesting their own rice, by far most of the supply still comes from independent farmers.

One of the farms growing sake rice for Yamaguchi's major breweries—among them Asahi Shuzo (Dassai), Sakai Shuzo (Gokyo), and Sumikawa Shuzo (Toyobijin)—is Fukumoto Nature Farm. The company is run solely by Fukumoto Takuo and his wife, who tend to ten hectares of organically grown rice in the small town of Tabuse. Fukumoto grows some table rice, but the majority of his fields are dedicated to rice for sake brewing, including the varieties Yamada Nishiki, Kame no O, Omachi, and Isehikari.

A field of Yamada Nishiki rice

"Organic results in lower yields, but I'm not in it for money," Fukumoto Takuo says. "It's just something fun for my retirement." Takuo was a high school teacher for thirty-two years before he inherited his father's fields, which he has expanded over the last ten years. "I started growing organic because my younger brother is allergic to agricultural chemicals, and at first it was just to try things out a little." Now, Fukumoto's entire production is officially certified organic, and he grows all his rice without any pesticides, herbicides, or artificial fertilizers. "The only thing I add to my fields is rice bran, since it came from the fields anyway, and some minerals that are JAS [Japan Agricultural Standards] certified."

As a result, Fukumoto's fields are full of life, and many of the creatures help keep his fields healthy. "*Tanishi* snails eat weeds and eat rice plants, too, but if you keep the water at the right level they mostly leave the rice alone," he says. Spiders and frogs help eat harmful bugs, as well, but one surprising result of organic farming is a surprisingly indirect resistance to pests. "In 2020, lots of fields around here were almost destroyed by *tobiiro unka* [brown planthoppers], but we had very little damage." He says this is because artificial fertilizers make plants excessively lush and soft, so they are easy to eat. "Organic rice plants have hard stalks and leaves, so the *unka* head to the softer plants and leave ours alone." Takuo says that he does get some pests in his fields, but he does not mind. "They eat their fill, and I still get my crop, so I am happy to try to coexist."

Even with those losses, Fukumoto rice is some of the best. "I started growing Yamada Nishiki in 2012. The first crop was rated *tokuto*, the second-highest rating. Now, about 80% of my crop is *tokuto* or *tokujo*, the highest ranking." He has also grown Omachi rice since 2018, a notoriously difficult rice most famously sourced from Okayama Prefecture, and again he has achieved very high ratings. "I sent my first crop to Sumikawa Shuzo, and they were shocked. It was all *tokuto*, and even the rice from Okayama isn't usually that high a grade. So, they said they would buy all I could grow."

Fukumoto is overjoyed by the reception his sake rice receives, but for him the reward is all in the bottle. "It's so great to meet up with the brewers and see how all that work ends up as sake. With table rice, you sell it, someone else eats it, and it's over. But with sake, you actually get to drink sake from your own fields, and it's so fun." Sake rice gets a higher selling price than food rice, so Fukumoto is hoping to expand production over the next few years, particularly of Yamada Nishiki.

At this point, Fukumoto says, his sake rice is all sold the minute it is harvested. "Apart from the standing orders for Dassai and Gokyo, and more recently Kinsuzume [Horie Sakaba], Sumikawa Shuzo has said they want to buy all the sake rice I have available. Sumikawa toji really wants to use local rice," he explains. Sake rice farmers plan out their crops a year or two in advance to make sure they plant enough to fill orders, which was a serious issue for farmers during the Covid-19 pandemic. Many sake breweries had stock back up, so some had to cancel standing rice orders, which left farmers with rice and no place to sell it. Fukumoto, though, was able to weather the storm due to the sheer quality of his harvest. "My table rice was worse off than sake rice. Restaurants weren't selling rice, so lots of my industry-intended rice backed up. But then people staying at home found they wanted better quality rice, so word of mouth spread, and people started buying directly from us."

Another source of local Yamada Nishiki is the Tsuru no Sato farm in the Yashiro district of Shunan. Tsuru no Sato is a purely local agricultural company that maintains, plants, and harvests fields for Yashiro farmers who have grown too old to continue on their own. They manage around 40 hectares of rice fields, and among them 2.1 are for Yamada Nishiki. Company president Onaka Iwao says they started planting Yamada Nishiki around 2010 at the specific request of Yamagata Toshiro, kuramoto of Yamagata Honten. "He first wanted to brew sake from our organic table rice, but it turned out to be too expensive. But he liked the idea of using locally grown rice, so he suggested we try planting Yamada Nishiki."

In the years since, Tsuru no Sato has adopted a low-chemical style of planting, using a mix of artificial and organic fertilizer, to grow its sake rice. The current head of the Yamada Nishiki section is thirty-four-year-old Jinda Shintaro. "I didn't intend to start growing sake rice when I joined the company, it just ended up that way. But I've been doing this for over a decade now, and I think I'm starting to get a sense of it." Tsuru no Sato still struggles to grow the highest grades of rice, *tokuto* or *tokujo*, but not for want of trying. "I've called farmers in Hyogo to ask about fertilizer timing and things, but they say the climate and soil is too different for them to know what to do here." This has not discouraged Onaka, however. "If President Yamagata wants to buy more, we'll plant more. It's a good cash crop!" he says.

As Yamaguchi's farmers continue to gain experience with this difficult rice, I fully expect the quality and output to grow. Soon, this prefecture may become known as much for its sake rice as for the delicious drink it becomes.

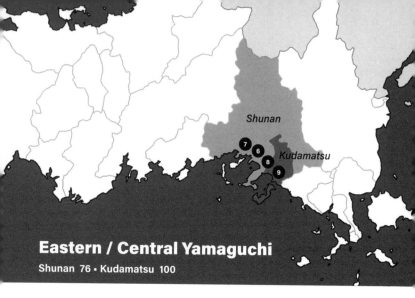

Eastern / Central Yamaguchi

Shunan 76 · Kudamatsu 100

SHUNAN (population 136,918 as of 2022) is in east-central Yamaguchi, stretching from the Seto Inland Sea to the Shimane border. It is in one sense the newest city in the prefecture, first appearing in 2003 after a municipal merger of the smaller communities of Tokuyama, Shinnan'yo, Kumage, and Kano. The name Shunan was chosen through public vote, but most of the local facilities still bear the old names. There is no Shunan Station, for example, so visitors get off the shinkansen at Tokuyama Station.

The individual towns that were merged into Shunan, however, all have long, deep histories. Tokuyama was capital of the Tokuyama Han domain from 1650, chosen primarily for its access to travel: a protected harbor, several reasonably large rivers for transport, and direct connection to the old San'yodo highway linking Kyoto with Shimonoseki. Even today, it has Yamaguchi's only major shinkansen station serving the highest-speed Nozomi and Sakura trains, as well as ports serving ferries to Kyushu and two points of access to the San'yo Expressway.

One mark of the area's historical significance is the concentration of sake breweries. There are three currently active breweries and several more that are still alive on paper but whose sake is made on contract elsewhere. One of the happier little sake facts about Shunan is that outstanding Hatsumomidi is a very short walk from Tokuyama Station and accepts tour requests, so visitors can easily get a look at a great Yamaguchi sake maker. The walk to this brewery passes through the commercial district just outside Tokuyama Station, where many of the restaurants and izakaya have local sake on the menu.

KUDAMATSU (population 57,294 as of 2022) is for all intents and purposes part of much larger Shunan, which almost completely surrounds it. The border between the two is so vague that no one from outside the city can identify where it is except when looking at addresses. However, the residents of Kudamatsu are fiercely independent—so much so that back in 2003, when Shunan was born through a merger of Tokuyama, Shinnan'yo, Kumage, and Kano, the residents of Kudamatsu refused to join unless everyone else accepted the Kudamatsu name and agreed to locating the city offices there. Clearly, the deal didn't go through, and today Kudamatsu remains an independent city.

Kudamatsu was the domain capital until the local Mori lord moved to Tokuyama in 1650 for better access to the port and highway there. Today Kudamatsu is relatively prosperous in its own right. It has several large factories, including a Hitachi plant where they build many of the trains and shinkansen cars you might ride on on your travels through western Japan.

Kudamatsu has but one sake brewery, Kinfundo Shuzo, located next to the ancient Hanaoka Hachimangu shrine.

6

Hatsumomidi
はつもみぢ

Founded 1819

Kuramoto	Harada Yasuhiro
Toji	Abe Mie (as of 2022)
Production	380 koku / 68.4 kiloliters
Main Label(s)	Harada 原田
Export Label(s)	Harada
Homepage	http://www.hatsumomidi.co.jp
Tours	available with reservations; no English support on-site

Hatsumomidi is perhaps the most accessible sake brewery in Yamaguchi. It is only a five-minute walk from Tokuyama Station, the prefecture's largest shinkansen station, so visitors coming via the San'yo Shinkansen line can stop by to see the brewery and use the direct-sales shop with little trouble. (In a departure from common romanization, the final *di* in the name is pronounced *ji*: *ha-tsu-mo-mi-ji*.)

You would be forgiven for walking right by it, though, because it barely looks like a sake brewery at all. "This building wasn't built to brew in. We were a beer distributor for twenty years, and so this was all just a warehouse and loading dock. But we're planning on redoing the whole place soon," says twelfth-generation family head and current kuramoto Harada Yasuhiro. The building is a testament to the turbulence of not only the brewery's history but of the industry's and Japan's as well.

When the brewery was founded in 1819, Japan was still in the

waning days of the Edo period, and the Tokuyama area was capital of the Tokuyama Han domain. There was a bustling city here already, and the brewery would have been supplying local shops and customers in an established commercial district. There are records indicating, in fact, that the Mori clan lords at Tokuyama Castle were avid fans of Harada Shinkura, as the brewery was known in those days.

The brewery thus knew success for most of its long history, until World War II. This area of Japan, with its many ports on the placid Seto Inland Sea, was the focus of rapid industrialization, and Tokuyama was an important manufacturing hub. That made it a prime target for attack, and in 1945 a bombing raid leveled much of the city—including the original Hatsumomidi brewery.

"It was rebuilt in the same place, but the cost was enormous," Harada says. To help fund reconstruction, the company signed a contract with Kyoto-based alcohol giant Takara Shuzo to act as a distributor for its sake, shochu, and beer. The added income helped the company survive, but as the sake market began to contract, Hatsumomidi came to depend more and more on the distribution business. Eventually, in 1985, the company stopped sake brewing altogether. "That's why this building just looks like a warehouse. It is! It was made for the beer distribution business," Harada says.

> One of the things that stand out the most about Hatsumomidi is the almost dizzying array of custom labels they produce.

Harada's father was running the business when they stopped brewing, and he remembers that it was a hard decision. "My father always wanted to restart brewing, but just couldn't. We were having sake brewed for us, then rebottling it and selling it. Our business was really just hauling drinks for other companies." When Harada was twenty-five, he returned to the company after university and began to feel that the sake side of the business, which was where his family had first started, was simply shameful. "I saw that the sake wasn't popular, and it wasn't selling. That led to it sitting there and getting old and becoming even less popular."

He decided to try to revive the brewing business himself. He took a training course from the National Research Institute of Brewing, then began test-brewing with a small batch of 300 kilograms of rice in December of 2005, a full twenty years since his family had stopped. It was a rocky start, but even so Harada decided after his third year to focus on the more tricky all-junmai brewing. He was helped in this by his champion palate. Harada has been Yamaguchi Prefecture's sake-tasting winner six times, and a finalist at the national competition as well.

Harada quickly developed a strong sense of what his sake should be. "I want it to be rice-focused and offer clarity and easy drinking. I have a few basic principles. We only use Yamada Nishiki for koji, and we press all our sake in a *fune* ("boat") press rather than the usual big accordion-style hydraulic machine. That reduces stress on the moromi and helps keep the flavor clean and smooth."

These principles also help maintain stability in the sake, because the brewery's water supply is itself slightly unstable. "We have a well on-site, which is probably why the brewery was first built here. But as the town grew around us, and the nearby factories expanded, the water quality just hasn't stayed good enough for sake." Instead, Hatsumomidi brings in water by tanker truck from a spring in the mountains, and the natural water quality shifts slightly with the seasons. Despite that, the brewery maintains its standards, and anyone who has tried Harada sake will see the results for themselves: a variety of styles, but all elegant and smooth, leaning toward the herbal and complex.

Now, after more than fifteen years of slow and steady growth, Harada is becoming a local and international favorite, although the kuramoto insists that Yamaguchi remains primary in his heart. "My goal from the start was to brew truly local sake. We only use rice grown here in Yamaguchi, and our main market is local, too." One of the things that stand out the most about Hatsumomidi is the almost dizzying array of custom labels they produce. It seems like every local *michi-no-eki* ("roadside stations" found along country highways selling local products) has a special sake brewed at Hatsumomidi just for them.

"We are happy to take on custom orders. We brew in small batches year-round, so it's pretty easy to work special brews into the schedule." Thus, labels like Kano Shizuku かの雫 (Droplets of Kano; Kano is a local farming village) or Nakasu Sake 泣かす酒 (made from table rice grown in the village of Nakasu) are brewed at the request of farming groups in local communities. "It's easy for us, and you should just see how happy the farmers are when they try sake made from their rice!"

This demonstrates how Harada has used the brewery's small scale for advantage. "The brewery layout doesn't allow for big tanks, so we have to keep lots of small ones going all the time," he says, and the result is not only the flexibility to adapt to requests but a great deal of varied experience in a short time. This has let Harada give his staff lots of intense training, and in recent years he has begun to leave more of the brewing work up to then-*fukutoji* (assistant brewmaster) Abe Mie, a working mother and smiling face of the brewery at sake events. The first batch Abe brewed entirely herself also happened to be the first time the brewery earned an award at the annual Japan Sake Awards, so Harada's sake seems to have a worthy successor already.

At the same time, Harada is supporting local education to help secure a future for the sake industry. He offers help to nearby Tabuse Agricultural High School, the only high school in Yamaguchi that teaches sake brewing to future generations of toji. Seishun 清春, another of Hatsumomidi's custom labels, is actually made by those students under guidance from Harada.

Hatsumomidi's period of dormancy is one that, sadly, is not so rare in the industry, so its revival and subsequent success offer a taste of hope for sake brewers everywhere. As this small Yamaguchi brewery continues to brew fantastic sake for more and more fans, we can only hope other breweries follow suit.

(Assistant brewmaster Abe Mie was appointed toji in the spring of 2022, between the writing of this section and publication.)

TOJI'S CHOICE SAKE

I talked to kuramoto and then-toji Harada Yasuhiro for this book in early 2021, right as he was rebranding and restyling his entire sake line. Naturally he wanted me to introduce one of his restyled versions, one he felt was most representative of the new image he wanted to

Harada Tokubetsu Junmai
Seimaibuai: 60%
Rice: Yamada Nishiki

bring to the Harada line. That image is, in a word, time. Hatsumomidi brews in small batches, year-round, meaning that Harada's sake is always fresh. As such, he felt it was important to express the moment of creation in each sake.

In other words, what he wants for his sake is a distinct freshness, a taste of its time and season of brewing. To do so, he says that he adjusts the yeast and the pasteurization to preserve a sensation of "nama"-ness, despite pasteurization.

In Harada Tokubetsu Junmai, I found that sense of freshness almost shocking. I had to ask several times to confirm that this new sake was not, in fact, an unpasteurized nama. It maintained a touch of mild carbonation and the nama feeling of zippy, almost tingling freshness, despite being pasteurized. Beyond that, it had a very bright, vibrant flavor and aroma, with notes of fruit, mochi rice cake, and clean acidity.

This is a delightful, refreshing sake that is a brilliant summer drink. The brilliant, juicy acidity takes on a bit more umami depth when warmed for winter drinking, but it still shines best chilled. It is a clear example that the balance, drinkability, and conscientious brewing that Harada is already known for continues to grow and evolve.

7

Nakashimaya Shuzojo

中島屋酒造場

Founded 1823

Kuramoto	Nakamura Nobuhiro
Toji	Nakamura Nobuhiro
Production	250 koku / 45 kiloliters
Main Label(s)	Kotobuki 寿, Nakashimaya 中島屋, Kanenaka カネナカ
Export Label(s)	Kotobuki, Nakashimaya, Kanenaka
Homepage	https://nakashimaya1823.jp/
Tours	available with reservations; no English support on-site

Nakashimaya Shuzojo is at the very western edge of Shunan, not far from National Highway 188, and it borders a major thoroughfare offering passersby a view of its newly remodeled Meiji-period facility. Nakashimaya is one of the few local breweries to survive from the Edo period without ever going dormant, although the years have not always been particularly kind.

The current president, Nakamura Nobuhiro, is the twelfth-generation head of his family and the eighth to run this sake brewery. He took over in 2021, as this book was being written, from his father Yujiro. The brewery founder, Kunigoro, was the fourth-generation family head and started brewing sake outside of what is now Shunan during the late Edo period. The brewery moved to its present site near the confluence of two rivers, the Tonda and the Fuji, some time in early Meiji. Today's kura is, then, not the

original, although it is still an impressive one hundred and fifty years old.

An underground flow from both rivers provides the kura's brewing water. As the water is medium hard, it isn't a notable influence on the sake, but it offers plenty of nutrients to support vigorous fermentation. That makes it easier to brew firmly structured, full-flavored sake, which is exactly the kind on which Nakashimaya has built its reputation.

Yujiro, already the kuramoto, took over the toji job as well after the company's previous Kumage toji retired at eighty years old, back in 1996. That was quite early on in the kuramoto/toji trend, making him a bit of a pioneer in the local industry. He has now given over brewing responsibility to his son Nobuhiro, but he still does some work in the brewery. Together, father and son make eighteen different brews spread across three labels.

The oldest label, Kotobuki 寿, is available only from local liquor shops that have long-standing relationships with Nakashimaya. Kotobuki's focus is on sake with broad appeal to the local market: futsushu and honjozo made with locally grown rice milled to 60%, and even some premium ginjo made with Yamaguchi's own Saito no Shizuku brewing rice. Sake bottled under the label Nakashimaya 中島屋 is for shops specializing in the *jizake*—or local craft sake—market and comprises special hand-crafted junmai ginjo, tokubetsu junmai, and other higher-end styles. This label is also where the brewery tries out new ideas, like the increasingly popular light summer sake. Finally, there is Kanenaka カネナカ, which features junmai sake made in the kimoto style.

This last label—Kanenaka—is one that I find particularly interesting. An increasing number of breweries are making kimoto these days, despite its more strenuous labor requirements and rather niche appeal. Kimoto is an old way of making the initial starter mash and in its archetypal form requires hours of backbreaking manual work mixing the initial batch of steamed rice, water, and yeast into a paste. The brewers allow naturally occurring lactic acid bacteria to propagate and make the mix acidic enough to prevent contamination from other bad bacteria. Many breweries find the result very attractive and appealing.

> Nakashimaya is also one of the increasingly rare Yamaguchi sake brewers still making futsushu. I ask about this, and their response is simple. "It still sells!"

In a way, this production method marks a return to Nakashimaya's roots. Kimoto was the standard brewing method until around 1910, when first the less labor-intensive but still slow and tricky yamahai method and then the faster and more stable sokujo method came on the scene. For the first eighty-seven years or so of the brewery's history, then, all of its sake would have been made with some version of the kimoto process. (Like most brewers, of course, Nakashimaya switched to the much faster, and much less labor intensive sokujo process soon after it appeared.)

However, the sake that results from kimoto starter is often quite full of character, with full-bodied acidity and a touch of almost wild, natural flavors. It has some very hardcore fans (I'm one of them!), but some find it a bit too "funky." That complex quality leads breweries to keep it around, despite the difficulties it presents, just to have some variety in their lineup.

Not many breweries have multiple kimoto versions in their regular lineup. Yet Nakashimaya has three under its Kanenaka label, which dates back to around 2002. "The kuramoto was looking for something to set us apart, and he liked kimoto, so we thought we'd give it a try," explains Nobuhiro. One of the more interesting things about this group of sake is how they are made. Instead of putting all of the burden on their few full-time workers, or hiring part-timers, the brewery calls on the community for help. Local sake shop owners, sake lovers, and really anyone they can convince to come all wake up early on a February morning, trek out to the brewery, and spend a day pounding tubs of rice with long wooden poles called *kai* in three- or four-hour shifts. It's hard, bone-numbing work, but no one seems to mind.

"If I can help keep them making Kanenaka, it's more than worth it," says Kawashima Keiji, manager of the (now, sadly defunct) Shunan sake bar Kokushu and a past participant in the task. "And it's not that bad, really. Our staff all helped out last time. You just end up with a few blisters!" Kawashima calls himself a hardcore Nakashimaya fan and says the Kanenaka line is fundamental to their brand. "Nakashimaya makes old fashioned sake with real flavor, and I'm glad they have Kanenaka in their lineup."

"We like sake that is flavorful and well structured, but doesn't weigh on the palate," Nobuhiro says. "We want drinkers to enjoy it in long sessions, not just sip at a single glass and feel like they've had enough." The kind of sake he aims for tends to be more acidic, which adds clean finishes with zip, and kimoto's lactic acid content is perfect for that. It's also an excellent sake for aging.

Nobuhiro says, "We age a lot of our sake. We have some regular labels that are aged three or five years. Kimoto results in sake that really stands up well." Aging sake to make what is called koshu is a small, but exciting, part of the modern sake industry. Most sake is intended to be drunk fresh after delivery, but laying it down to mature can bring out new levels of depth and balance. However, sake can be unstable, and sometimes aging is unpredictable. The higher acidity and more robust flavors of kimoto sake make it a bit more resilient and thus offers a more reliable result.

In a way, this production method marks a return to Nakashimaya's roots. Kimoto was the standard brewing method until around 1910, when first the less labor-intensive but still slow and tricky yamahai method and then the faster and more stable sokujo method came on the scene.

Nakashimaya is also one of the increasingly rare Yamaguchi sake brewers still making futsushu. I ask about this, and their response is simple. "It still sells!" Kotobuki has been a local favorite for almost two hundred years, and even during the postwar years, when so-called "tripled sake," or *sanzoshu*, made with vast amounts of added sweeteners, distilled alcohol, and flavoring, was the norm, its fans didn't abandon it. Now, nothing is added to the sake except brewer's alcohol, and like some other Yamaguchi futsushu makers Nakashimaya use only locally grown rice. "We make sake for flavor, but we still want to respect the ingredients."

Concern like that tells in the final product. Nakashimaya's

Kotobuki Josen is a surprisingly crisp, clean finishing futsushu, especially for a brewery that once had a reputation for *nojun amakuchi* (richly sweet), even when it went directly against the trends. Yujiro explains how "in the 1990s, when *tanrei karakuchi* (light, crisp sake) was the rage, we were selling sweet. The average SMV [Sake Meter Value] back then was +5 [a bit dry], but our Josen was -7 [rather sweet]. Nowadays, as we make less futsushu and more kimoto, we've evened out and our average SMV overall is around 0, but we were always a very sweet sake maker."

Nakashimaya still does not let trends guide their overall business too much. Currently, Nakashimaya's production is 80% junmai and only 20% aruten, but they are not planning on going any further. Nobuhiro says, "Junmai is more expensive for the customers, especially for our long-time fans who've come to love our aruten sake. I don't see us changing any time soon."

TOJI'S CHOICE SAKE

It took a while for the father and son brewing duo to choose a sake to introduce here. Their core style lies in the kimoto Kanenaka range, but they can also create more aromatic, delicate sake in daiginjo and junmai daiginjo expressions.

In the end, they went with their Nakashimaya Junmai Ginjo. Their reasoning was that this is the clearest expression of its ingredients, which for this particular sake is Yamada Nishiki grown in the nearby Tokuji district of Yamaguchi City.

I initially tried this sake chilled to around 15 degrees Celsius in a wine glass. It is fragrant, with notes of ripe red apple and overripe banana, and a green herbal note underpinning them both. The initial attack is a bright, crisp sweetness that fades to a pleasant umami on the sides of the tongue, which washes away with a clean, acidic astringency.

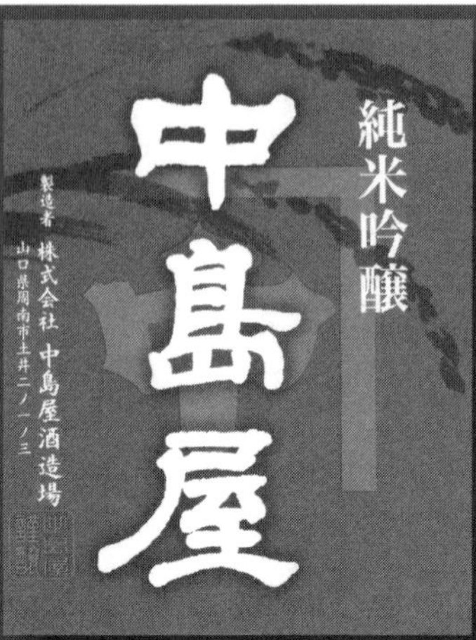

純米吟醸

中島屋

製造者　株式会社　中島屋酒造場
山口県周南市上村二ノ一ノ三

Nakashimaya Junmai Ginjo
Seimaibuai: 50%
Rice: Yamada Nishiki

The sake has clear depth, defined by a firm structure of umami, but strikes me as entirely elegant and refined. I would have expected Nakashimaya to create what is usually called an *aji gin*, a flavor-focused ginjo that aims for rich, *nojun* character, but this is quite aromatic and leans toward delicacy. At the same time, it had the backbone to stand up to a steak dinner, and indeed the big umami flavors of the grilled meat melded nicely with the sake's flavor mix.

This is an outstanding example of Yamaguchi brewers taking Yamaguchi rice and creating a ginjo that can stand up to any in the country. It is not, perhaps, as clear and pure an evocation of Nakashimaya's defining style as you find in the Kanenaka labels, but it will not disappoint those looking for a sophisticated premium sake that presents more than just a pleasant sip. Chilled, that is.

Heated, though, it wakes up. The delicacy retreats before an assertive acidity and lets the umami shine through in an entirely new, mouthwatering way. This is the Nakashimaya sake I know and love, the one that begs to be warmed up and sipped on a cold autumn evening.

Yamagata Honten
山縣本店

Founded 1875

Kuramoto	Yamagata Toshiro
Toji	Ogasawara Mitsuhiro
Production	600 koku / 108 kiloliters
Main Label(s)	Kaori かほり, Bouchotsuru 防長鶴, Moriko 毛利公
Export Label(s)	Kaori, Bouchotsuru, Moriko
Homepage	https://yamagt.jp/en/
Tours	available with reservations; English explanations offered

Yamagata Honten sakagura is in the Kume district of Shunan City, in a rapidly growing residential neighborhood just a stone's throw from the San'yo Shinkansen tracks. The kura has been changing and growing along with the neighborhood, with a new label and renovations inside to match its premium aspirations. There are no new buildings, but the interior of the main kura, built in 1875, has been modernized to keep up with demand driven by the Yamaguchi Sake Revolution.

Yamagata Toshiro is the fourth-generation kuramoto of Yamagata Honten and has been running the brewery for nearly forty-five years. This period just happens to be one of the most volatile in sake's history, and he has overseen a huge shift in not only his own business, but the industry as a whole.

"When I started here, sake making was still under the postwar system, so rice was rationed. We could only use the rice allotted to us, and smaller sakagura outside the big areas of Nada or Niigata

had to work with that to keep up with production," Yamagata says. The upshot of that was a reliance on the highly adulterated *sanzoshu* process—adding massive amounts of brewer's alcohol, acidifiers, and sweeteners to triple production. At the same time, small breweries often had trouble selling under their own names, so much of their production was rerouted to Hiroshima, Osaka, or the major makers in Hyogo for sale under other labels. "Only a couple of kura here in Yamaguchi were able to actually sell all their sake under their own names."

Rice rationing eventually ended and production went up dramatically, but around the same time demand started to drop. Major makers could now make enough sake to cover their markets. "We could make all the sake we wanted, but the national brands who already had major facilities no longer needed production from outside. Sales really took a nosedive."

Yamaguchi's sake brewers had been treading water and trying to recover after World War II, but now even that was growing difficult. From such circumstances Yamaguchi's sake innovations were born.

"I came in about forty-five years ago, when my father was still kuramoto. He was sick and needed someone to manage the business. We were in serious trouble, I have to be honest. I had to look for a way to find new customers. I wanted something that young people and women would drink." Seeing that beer was replacing sake as the drink of choice, he had an inspiration. "The way people were drinking beer, to relax and such, was easier when it was cold. People loved cold beer. Sake was either hot *kanzake* or *hiya*—which meant room temperature back then. But electric refrigerators were finally common enough that people could drink cold beer at home. Why not cold sake?"

Yamagata set out to develop a sake that was made to be drunk cold, one that was more aromatic, with fruity overtones and less umami heaviness so it would be easier to drink for a wider range of consumers. His efforts came to fruition in 1984 with the release of Kaori, a name reminiscent of the Japanese word for "aroma." Kaori was the first sake meant to be drunk cold in Japan, and according to Yamagata helped spark the current cold-drinking ginjo revolution. It was a hit and quickly overtook the brewery's previous mainstay, Bouchotsuru, in sales; around twenty years ago the kura retired the older label entirely.

With the success of Kaori, Yamagata Honten's future was assured. But the kuramoto has continued to pursue innovation. This is, he says, what sake has always been about. "Sake has two thousand years of history, and it has always changed. There has always been innovation in sake, and there always will be. Innovation in production, in packaging, in drinking."

Yamagata has always valued locality, too. "It's only lately that we've started to realize how important terroir is in sake making. We always knew that local sake and local food worked together well.

And we always wanted to use local products, but now we recognize how important that connection is in our sake." Yamagata uses mostly Yamaguchi-grown sake rice, primarily Yamada Nishiki and now Saito no Shizuku; its shochu distilling operation also uses only Yamaguchi-grown sweet potatoes and rice.

Toji Ogasawara Mitsuhiro, a native of nearby Shimane Prefecture, actually came to work at Yamagata Honten because of the shochu. "I wasn't really interested in sake at first. I was working in a restaurant in Hiroshima when a customer asked me if I wanted to come help out at a sake brewery," he explains. He spent three years at Enoki Shuzo, a sake brewery in Kure, Hiroshima, which makes the incredibly rare *kijoshu* style of sake that uses previous batches of sake in lieu of some brewing water.

"I spent three years at Enoki, and then the shochu boom started. I thought about heading down to Kyushu to work at a distillery and learn to make it there, but then I learned that there was this sake brewery in Yamaguchi that also made sweet potato shochu. So, I came here." He started out solely on the distillery side, but since Yamagata is so small, he soon started helping out with sake brewing. Nine years after he joined the company, he became toji. "I didn't think it would be something you could just become like that, but here I am. And then I went and married the kuramoto's daughter!" In doing so, not only did Ogasawara become a full member of the Yamagata family, but he also helped assure the future of the brewery.

With an immense grin, Yamagata says, "I was worried, actually, because my son said he wasn't interested in running the business, and my daughter was going to go to America to study. I asked her to wait a while and help out, but then I hired our new toji, and a miracle happened! They fell in love and got married. So now she's ready to be the fifth-generation kuramoto."

The family feeling within the kura comes through with every

visit. Yamagata's wife, Yasuko, and daughter, Ogasawara Misako, work at the kura and offer guided tours of the facilities in English. The family bonds are also reflected in the trust that Yamagata has placed in his toji, who does not have the kind of background most others do.

> Yamagata set out to develop a sake that was made to be drunk cold, one that was more aromatic, with fruity overtones and less umami heaviness so it would be easier to drink for a wider range of consumers. His efforts came to fruition in 1984 with the release of Kaori, a name reminiscent of the Japanese word for "aroma."

"We just relaunched our original label Bouchotsuru and I have big hopes for that. It was actually all Ogasawara's idea. He started after our old toji, the last Kumage toji, quit. He was seventy, and in poor health. Ogasawara is young and has lots of ideas. He's already changed things a lot." And Bouchotsuru does mark a distinct change. The new, striking label has come to dominate Yamagata Honten's sake branding and is winning awards at home and abroad.

I asked Ogasawara about his own ideas for this label. "First of all, it's our junmai-only label. We still have some aruten sake under the others, but this is going to stay junmai, premium only." Yamagata will likely never go fully junmai, as many others have, because not only do they still sell a lot of the cheaper grades of sake, but they also supply futsushu to dormant breweries that want to keep their labels active. It is part of the business, and business is relatively good. "I brew sake for a lot of other labels, but with Bouchotsuru I can focus exactly on what I want. I like clean, crisp finishes, without a lot of heavier elements. Lots of depth, but still dry." This premium-only label is a clear shot at staying on top of the Yamaguchi Sake Revolution.

Yamagata has been a part of this revolution from the beginning and is happy to share his view on how it came to be. "Of course, Dassai has been a big influence. It brought a lot of attention from outside the prefecture on Yamaguchi sake, and from inside it showed people the possibilities of the market. But you know, one thing that really has been important is that when the market began contracting, all of us small brewers had the same problem. We couldn't compete with the national labels in production, so what could we compete in? There was only one choice: small-batch, hand-crafted premium sake. And because all of us were so small, it was fairly easy to change. We were in a unique position, because of the lack of a single style and such. It wasn't any kind of foresight or anything; we had no idea that premium sake would start to take off. It's like a miracle. That's the only word that fits."

He points out that this is exactly what made Dassai successful. "They came in right after I made Kaori, helping to create the idea of cold sake, and started making their junmai daiginjo. They'd lost their toji and they had nowhere else to turn, so they just went pure premium. And look at them now!"

He is also optimistic about the future. "I think it's going to go well for now. One thing that this success has done is bring lots more young people back into sake making. We've had several kura that were dormant, or close to it, that have been revived by younger members of the family coming back to Yamaguchi and making them into something new." This describes outstanding breweries like Ohmine Shuzo, Abu no Tsuru Shuzo, and Shintani Shuzo.

In the end, I think what best encapsulates the Yamaguchi sake power, and the heart of Yamagata Honten's brewing, is expressed in a final message from Ogasawara toji: "We sake brewers are really just regular people who want to make the very best drink we can. The true goal here is for people to enjoy the sake. That's all I want, anyway."

TOJI'S CHOICE SAKE

Bouchotsuru
Junmai Daiginjo
Seimaibuai: 40%
Rice: Saito no Shizuku

The Bouchotsuru label represents Yamagata Honten's premium, junmai-only brewing selection, and this daiginjo is the pinnacle of that label. Toji Ogasawara Mitsuhiro says that this is the closest he has come to his ideal sake: clean, clear, medium-dry sake that brings the depth of the rice's natural flavor to bear without being overwhelming.

If that is true, then I can say that I like his ideal. This sake starts out with a bright, vibrant aroma. It brings clear green apple notes and almost tart berry to the nose, with grassy, herbal hints to keep it interesting.

The first sip again brings berry sweetness, but without excessive acidity to make it tart. There are hints of peach and sweet rice, with almost a touch of vanilla, but none of it is overly sweet. It maintains a solid, medium-dry core with a good umami understructure.

The finish is very quick and clean, with a hint of astringency lingering to keep the mouth fresh. Overall, this sake almost presents like a medium-dry white wine. The mild acidity and astringency do not dominate the flavors but keep it fresh and crisp, evoking the clarity that Ogasawara says he strives for.

This sake is best very mildly chilled, I think, and is quite nice with simply flavored meals like grilled salmon or a buttery pasta.

connections

Sake Shops and Bars

Yamamotoya Liquor Shop

The sake industry encompasses people and businesses far beyond the producers. The relationships between sake brewers and sake retailers is fundamental to the success of any sake brewery, although Japan's rather intricate liquor licensing laws mean that the lines between producer, wholesaler, and retailer are fuzzy at best. Breweries can sell directly to customers, and businesses can—and do—source their sake from retail outlets as well as B2B wholesalers or even directly from breweries.

The general consumer market is currently dominated by chain stores, including supermarkets and convenience stores, but surprisingly, the restaurant liquor supply segment is overwhelmingly filled by local sake shops. Small neighborhood liquor stores might not see much foot traffic, but their delivery vans are sure to be out carrying wares to trade customers on a daily basis. That focus is generally what keeps most shops alive in the face of big tent competition, but during the Covid-19 pandemic everyone struggled. The enormous drop in restaurant and bar sales hit not only the sake makers but the sake sellers as well, and many local neighborhood liquor stores were on the brink of bankruptcy.

Still, the relationship between breweries and liquor shops is a vital one that has in many ways shaped the path of the industry. The spread of the junmai boom can in many ways be attributed to Tokyo-area liquor shops encouraging their suppliers to follow the growing demand, but at the same time some breweries had difficulty exploring innovative ideas due to resistance from the local retailers they depended on.

What does it take to build and

maintain the relationships that put a liquor retailer in that kind of position? As Yamamoto Tadaaki of Yamamotoya Liquor and Gifts in Shunan's Shinnan'yo district explains, "Most local sake shops deal directly with breweries. That way you can visit them directly and get a first-hand sense of the people who are making the sake, the place they make it, and the care that goes into it." The connections are not always easy to make, though. "Sometimes I go to a brewery to ask if we can carry their sake and get turned down. But I don't give up, and I work on building trust through visits."

That trusting relationship is vital on both sides. Some sake brewers insist on visiting potential dealers as well, to make sure of the quality of their management, facilities, and even atmosphere.

Yamamoto himself is not only a sake dealer; he is also a sake sommelier and educator who helps run classes to encourage more local sake fans to get engaged in the beverage. "I hold sake-tasting sessions to guide people in understanding sake mostly just for fun, but also to add a little education to the process." He also holds basic certification classes to encourage more advanced sake drinkers to study the production and culture around sake. "My work in passing on the history and culture of sake has no end goal. It's something I believe in, and will do until I die!"

Naturally, Yamamoto carries a number of local sake breweries in his shop. "Yamaguchi has breweries of all sizes, with such unique style and so much creativity. . . . I want to let the world know about the joys of local sake from Yamaguchi, and all of Japan."

Kokushu Sake Bar

Kokushu was, until spring of 2022, a sake specialty bar near Tokuyama Station, and it exemplified what I think a sake bar should be. Rather than being a typical service bar, it had a wall of refrigerators full of sake from all over Japan for self-service. Above each refrigerator was a sign listing the name

Signage of the Kokushu Sake Bar

an education center. It hosted events for local sake brewers to come and meet drinkers to educate them about their sake and how to drink it. Manager Kawashima Keiji also educated customers, particularly younger ones, and guided them in finding a bottle that meets their needs. He considered it part of his duty as a sake lover to bring new fans into the fold.

The connections Kawashima helped build were fostered by location. The bar was only a few minutes' walk from Hatsu-momidi, home of the Harada label, and kuramoto Harada Yasuhiro was a frequent face at events. Kawashima, an inveter-ate fan of local brewery Naka-shimaya, promoted those and other local brews at every chance.

Kokushu stocked outstanding brands from all over Japan like Kaiun, Tamagawa, and Izumi-bashi, but favored the richer fla-vors close to home. He makes sure his suppliers stock those refrigerators with all the Yama-guchi favorites, and plenty of lesser-known labels as well. In addition to Taka, Gangi, Tenbi,

of the liquor shop that supplied it. Yamamotoya is one of those shops and supplies the Kokushu refrigerator with outstanding local sake labels like Tenbi from Choshu Shuzo, or Nagayama Honke Shuzojo's Taka.

Beyond being a place to drink sake, though, Kokushu was

and Dassai, the refrigerators usually held Bouchotsuru, Choyo Fukumusume, Wakamusume, and more.

Kawashima, who now manages a nearby restaurant, has worked in the hospitality industry for over thirty years and says that the unique experience of Kokushu was always his dream. "I wanted people who came to leave liking sake more than when they walked in," he says. "Our system let people try and compare all kinds of sake, so they develop a better sense of the flavor, and learn what they like."

This was also the reason behind all those events. "Shunan has three sake breweries now, and we hosted all three for events. It helped bring the customers closer to local sake, and deepens their love of the drink," Kawashima says, reflecting his attachment to the local industry. "Every one of Yamaguchi's sake breweries is so distinct, and has such clear identity, that it's easy to find something to match any taste."

Kawashima is now manager at Akaoni Bunten, a small evening dining spot that offers up a fine place to drink but is yet to fill the greater social role that a great sake bar really can play. His shuttering of Kokushu in 2022 represented something greater than just the closing of another bar during the intractable Covid-19 pandemic. It signaled something sad about the place of sake in Japan's drinking culture itself. That is because, despite the unique, almost ideal sake-drinking experience that Kokushu offered, it was still unable to survive the ever-downward slide of the demand for sake among the Japanese.

9

Kinfundo Shuzo
金分銅酒造

Founded 1900

Kuramoto	Maito Toshiko
Toji	Hirata Eiji (as of 2018)
Production	not disclosed
Main Label(s)	Akatsuki 婀伽坏, Ikuyamakawa 幾山河, Kinfundo 金分銅
Export Label(s)	none
Homepage	http://ww52.tiki.ne.jp/~kinfundou-sa/shin.html
Tours	not offered

Kinfundo Shuzo's time-worn sales shop faces a residential street, but to reach the entrance to the brewing buildings you must go up a cobblestone lane leading to Hanaoka Hachimangu shrine. The entrance to this road is guarded by the shrine's towering stone *torii* gate, although the shrine itself is still a few minutes' walk away. This location visibly demonstrates the connections between Kinfundo and the shrine, which is also revealed by any quick perusal of the brewery's website or its labels. Another example: Kinfundo draws its brewing water from the same source as the spring that feeds the shrine's sacred basin.

The brewing water here is relatively soft, as in fact most sake-brewing water is. Kinfundo quite publicly credits the water and its source, even offering it for tasting on the one day a year they are open to the public. The goal is to show how the water influences the finished product, helping create a smooth, delicate mouthfeel even with the depth of flavor that Kinfundo sake offers.

This water also inspired the name of Kinfundo's *nojun karakuchi* (rich and dry) brew, Akatsuki (made with Saito no Shizuku rice). An *akatsuki* is a cup used to draw water from a sacred well, or *akai*, like those found outside Buddhist temples or Shinto shrines. Since the brewery's water and Hanaoka Hachimangu shrine's well water are the same, this name helps remind drinkers that this sake is bringing that same "sacred" water to their cups.

Kinfundo is currently run by Maito Toshiko, one of three women heading sake breweries in Yamaguchi. She is the fourth-generation owner and keeps her family business alive and relevant by building on the firm local market base with newer, premium styles.

As a small, unpretentious brewery, Kinfundo shies away from attention. It does not offer open tours and avoids the media. The kuramoto even refused to offer any interviews for this book. My visits have thus been limited to the yearly open house (currently suspended due to the pandemic), where the kuramoto's sister shows local visitors through the three warehouse-style buildings and then guides everyone through a tasting of Kinfundo's various products and the odd stroll to their shop.

On those rare visits, walking through Kinfundo feels like being inside a brewing museum. The dim interior is filled with aged tanks and now unused equipment, including massive ceramic bottles once used for sake distribution in the early 1900s. There is a sunken, stone-lined storage space that was once cooled by underground streams but now has been retrofitted with refrigeration systems, and all of it is surrounded by exposed wooden beams that tell a story of age and long use. It is a beautiful place, full of the touches of tradition that are all too often cast off by breweries looking to modernize.

As Yamaguchi's sake brewing has improved and its brewers come to support each other in the challenges of premium-sake brewing, Kinfundo has joined in and broadened production into junmai and ginjo styles. Nevertheless, they still use many older, less efficient methods to create their unique flavor. They use a traditional wooden *fune* press—essentially a large wooden box with a big hydraulic press on the top—rather than the newer accordion-style Yabuta machines, and they make all their koji, even for the simple table sake *josen futsushu*, purely by hand. It is a struggle, as their staff is aging, but they are a bastion of traditional flavors in a changing world.

Kinfundo's most distinctive label, Ikuyamakawa, is easy to spot at local supermarkets because of its dried-bamboo-skin wrapping. It bears the prominent characters 地酒, *jizake*, written even larger than the name. The term means "local sake," and the junmai inside is the archetype of old-fashioned Yamaguchi flavor: sweet, rich, full, and unabashedly *nojun*. This particular label is a testament to Yamaguchi brewing history as well. The story I heard is that, before marriage brought her here to Kudamatsu, the kuramoto's mother's family operated a brewery on the nearby island of Suo Oshima.

That brewery, unfortunately long closed, was the original home of Ikuyamakawa. Now, Maito keeps her mother's legacy alive with this traditional product.

Kinfundo is a strong supporter of local sourcing, using Yamaguchi-grown Yamada Nishiki in its premium sake as well as Yamaguchi's original sake rice Saito no Shizuku. This is a difficult rice to work with, by all accounts, and using it for a hundred percent of a brewing batch instead of the common practice of using Yamada Nishiki for the rice koji is something even better-equipped breweries hesitate to do. Despite this challenge, Kinfundo's take is clean and modern, yet still an example of the full-flavored style that this brewery does so well.

Kinfundo preserves one other fading tradition: the toji system. Traditionally, sake brewing was done in the winter by rice farmers in the off season. Those farmers formed the groups that became toji guilds and would travel to whatever sake brewery had hired them with their own teams of other farmer/brewers to live and work at the brewery during the season on a yearly contract basis. This is called the *toji seido*, or toji system, in Japan, and it is almost dead. Now the toji is usually either a locally based full-time employee of the brewery or a family member of the kuramoto (if not the kuramoto personally), and living at the brewery itself is almost unheard of. Kinfundo is the only sake brewery in Yamaguchi that preserves this system. Its toji is part of the Hiroshima guild and comes in winter to brew the season's sake while staying on the premises.

Kinfundo does not currently export any sake, and the only place to visit is its on-site shop. However, the nearby grocery and department stores all have a full selection of Kinfundo sake—including the striking Ikuyamakawa junmai in its bamboo wrapping, which makes a great Yamaguchi souvenir.

AUTHOR'S CHOICE SAKE

Akatsuki Honjozo
Seimaibuai: 60%
Rice: Saito no Shizuku

Akatsuki may not be the top of Kinfundo Shuzo's premium class, but it is a perfect example of the balance of old-fashioned sake flavor and modern trends in their lineup. First off, it is a honjozo, which is the opposite of a trendy sake these days. Next, the label calls it an *umakara* sake, meaning it is brewed to emphasize the umami notes of the rice, while not being overly sweet. This is a richer, or *nojun*, expression that ignores the recent trends toward light, crisp, dry sake. It is also made 100% from Yamaguchi's local Saito no Shizuku rice, a relative rarity even in Yamaguchi—most breweries use Yamada Nishiki for the koji with the more difficult rice varieties like Saito no Shizuku used for the main *kakemai* mashing rice. At the same time, Akatsuki offers nods to modern trends with big, bold label designs and a focus on quick, clean finishes rather than lingering dryness.

The result is a big, rich sake that carries the taste of an almost bygone day. There is no delicate berry fruitiness here, rather the kind of hefty umami and mouth cleansing acidity that absolutely begs for heating. This is a junmai that absolutely shines with traditional Japanese dishes like *oden* or yakitori, especially on a cold winter evening and heated up to a good 45 degrees Celsius.

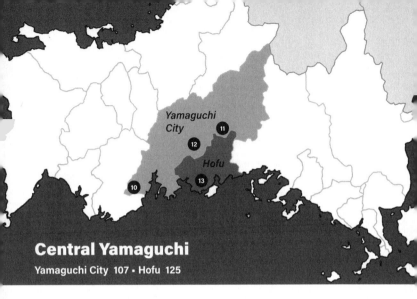

Yamaguchi
City

11

12

Hofu

13

10

Central Yamaguchi

Yamaguchi City 107 · Hofu 125

YAMAGUCHI CITY (population 192,298 as of 2022) is the modern prefectural capital, but before that it was the central capital of the Nagato and Suo provinces under the Ouchi clan, and later the Mori.

The Ouchi clan was famously wealthy and worked hard to make their capital a cultural center for western Japan. The foreign trade they cultivated and their fascination with continental culture resulted in considerable Chinese influence on the city. Ouchi Masahiro (1446–95) invited famed artist Sesshu to come for a period, and many of his works are now on display in various museums around the prefecture. Similarly, the openness of Ouchi Yoshitaka (1507–51) encouraged Portuguese Jesuit missionary Francis Xavier to spend considerable time here, a stay commemorated by the St. Francis Xavier Memorial Church.

The Mori clan replaced the Ouchi not long before the Edo period arrived in the early 1600s. They originally built their capital at Hagi but moved back to Yamaguchi in 1863, shortly before the Meiji Restoration that led to the end of feudal reign in Japan. The Mori leaders brought with them a cadre of intellectuals and budding politicians to plot the revolution right here in the city, and many of those men went on to lead the country as it built its new democracy after the Restoration.

This area's central role in government also gives it a long history as a sake center, although it has sadly lost most of its brewing power. Of the three breweries still listed in Yamaguchi City, one is actually not a brewery at all—Yamashiroya has its sake made by another brewer, although they do buy and ship their own rice, and even their own water, for the brewing, so they get special mention in this book. The company otherwise exists solely as a liquor shop on the main shopping arcade north of Yamaguchi Station, with many of the brewery's once-used barrels and signs on display there. The other two Yamaguchi breweries are found far outside the city proper, so access to them is trickier.

HOFU (population 113,866 as of 2022) is one of Yamaguchi's hidden surprises. With no shinkansen station or airport, this low-key little city can be difficult to reach, but for those who make the effort to get there the payoff is enormous. It served as the capital of Suo Province and was the seat of the local branch of the Mori clan's power for decades. Its resulting concentration of incredible temples, shrines, and gardens overshadows even Yamaguchi City's. Check the end of this book for specific travel information.

There is currently only one sake brewery in Hofu, Takeuchi Shuzo, but the city itself has been granted something special: official doburoku production-area status. Doburoku is rough, unfiltered/unpressed sake that has a long history as, basically, homebrew. It was long made by farmers for their community, and now, in Hofu, they can do it again.

Kanemitsu Shuzo

金光酒造

Founded 1926

Kuramoto	Kanemitsu Akio
Toji	none
Production	300 koku / 54 kiloliters
Main Label(s)	Santoka 山頭火, Muroka 夢露香
Export Label(s)	Santoka
Homepage	http://www.santouka.com/index.html
Tours	available with reservations; no English support on-site

Kanemitsu Shuzo is located in a nebulous gray zone between suburban and rural Japan. It is only ten minutes' drive from Shin-Yamaguchi shinkansen station, which is surrounded by chain stores and restaurants, and the brewery building faces a large public elementary school. But to one side, rice fields stretch out to the distant tree line. This is the Kamikagawa district of Yamaguchi City, home to perhaps the most intense expression of "local production for local consumption" I have ever seen.

Kanemitsu's main label is Santoka, but a banner out front proudly displays the name Kaho no Sato. When I ask about this name, one I'd not seen before, kuramoto Kanemitsu Akio nodded. "A local sake shop had the idea, and we just went along. That was seventeen years ago, and we still make it every year." And just what is that idea?

Kaho no Sato is a sake brewed from sake rice planted, grown, and harvested by the local community in fields within sight of the brewery. Planting and harvesting are accompanied by local

festivals, and everyone helps out with the work. Even the name, which loosely translates to "village of Ka River rice," was decided by a public vote. After the harvest, Kanemitsu turns the rice into a brew fitting the year's harvest—anything from a creamy nigori to a junmai daiginjo. The sake is then sold only at local shops. There is no way to even see a bottle except by visiting Kamikagawa, and that will likely never change. "Really, it's not even our sake," Kanemitsu says. "It all belongs to the sake sellers. But it has worked out so well, we see no need to try changing it."

This kind of local cooperation permeates the brewery. All of the rice it uses comes from local Yamaguchi fields. All of the staff members are from the neighborhood. And there is no toji here, which is a rarity at a sake brewery this size. "We do it all together. Everything is decided as a group—the schedule, the division of roles, the styles of sake we brew." I express doubt about this. Surely, as kuramoto without a toji, he is the one to decide what gets done? "I make suggestions, but all the decisions come to a vote. We even decide the label designs as a group."

Anyone familiar with the state of the sake industry can most likely imagine how things got to be this way. Kanemitsu did have a traditional toji, of course, from the Kumage Toji guild. He got too old to continue the work, however, and there was no one to take over after he left. Kanemitsu himself had never worked that much in the brewery, and although he had a grasp of the basics he was not ready to take over. The former toji's closest helpers had also mostly left, so the staff that did remain were relatively inexperienced, and no one wanted to take on the responsibility. So, they cooperated. People did what they knew how to do and more or less had everything covered. As time went on, Kanemitsu and his staff became more capable. "Now, we have five people working in the brewery, and two in the office. There are two of us in charge of brewing, two in charge of pressing, and one in charge of bottling. But we all do everything, actually." The day I went to visit, sixty-eight-year-old Kanemitsu had just spent the morning helping to bottle sake, and his afternoon was given to paperwork and dealing with me.

"It works out, mostly. The hardest part is when someone leaves. When you have such a small crew, where everyone is part of the work, a single person's experience is really valuable. Losing anyone can throw off the whole process," he says. Looking around, though, I was happy to see most of the staff was younger than me, and they were all moving about with confidence and the look of experience. There was also a lot of new equipment, including refrigerated rooms for pressing and for moromi. The brewery appears to have a future for now, I say.

"I hope so. This Covid thing has been hard, but not as hard as it could have been. Yamaguchi accounts for nearly all our sales, and probably 80% are just in Yamaguchi City and Hofu. So, sales went down, but not as bad as the breweries that focus on the big cities outside the prefecture." He said that one interesting change was an increase in interest from overseas. "We've started getting just a few orders from Taiwan and China, so that's good. It's still really small, but who knows?"

One other sign that Kanemitsu is looking forward is a complete restyling of their sake's look, bringing modern design to a lineup that at the moment is decidedly traditional. "This is actually kind of funny. We did all of this years ago, but to actually bring the new labels to the market we feel like we need to do it all at once. Which means we want to sell out of all the old product at the same time, and there's never been a clear time to do it! And so, we just keep using the old designs," the kuramoto says, with a weary laugh.

Those labels all feature some connection to the Santoka name. There is no talk of changing that, even with the new designs. The sake is named after Taneda Santoka, penname of early-twentieth-century Japanese poet Taneda Shoichi, who was born in nearby Hofu. Santoka is famous for his free-verse haiku, and almost as famous for his love of drink. He and his father once opened a sake brewery in what is now Hofu. Although the business did not succeed, the Santoka license and facility eventually ended up with the current Kanemitsu Shuzo.

Kanemitsu takes this historic connection very seriously. The poet's portrait adorns many of their labels, and there are books of Santoka's poetry piled up in the kura's main office. "He loved sake, you know. And we like to make the kind of sake he would have drunk!" Kanemitsu says. The brewery's online shop even attributes their Kurade Genshu label's kick-in-the-teeth robustness (they call it *kitsui*—harsh—in the tasting notes) to Santoka's tastes. "This is just the kind of *kitsui* sake Santoka loved!" it says. I can't speak to that personally, but it is certainly the kind of full-bodied, hefty sake that I personally find a refreshing return to tradition in today's fruitiness-focused sake market.

BREWER'S CHOICE SAKE

Santoka Junmai Daiginjo
Seimaibuai: 40%
Rice: Saito no Shizuku

If Kanemitsu Shuzo's many different sake have a defining characteristic, it is the one summed up in the Japanese phrase *nomigotae*. The term is difficult to translate concisely, but it conveys a sense of heft, of a drink that asserts itself on the palate. Santoka Junmai Daiginjo conveys real *nomigotae*. It is not a delicate, aromatic flower of a sake; it is one that carries itself with confidence and force.

Which is not to say that it is overly heavy, or even rich. It starts off with the kind of aromas you would expect from a premium daiginjo, with notes of simple fruit like apple and banana, filled out with a touch of citrus sourness and warm vanilla.

The initial flavor is richly sweet with touches of honey and ice cream, but it quickly fades into a light finish with a gentle lingering umami. The flavor is big but not cloying, and the acidity hits the side of the tongue in a pleasing, mouthwatering way.

This sake is a lovely expression of the way a junmai daiginjo can show both elegance and heft, preserving the traditional role of sake as a meal drink while still rewarding slow, contemplative sipping.

Shintani Shuzo
新谷酒造

Founded 1927

Kuramoto	Shintani Yoshinao
Toji	Shintani Fumiko
Production	80 koku / 14.4 kiloliters
Main Label(s)	Wakamusume わかむすめ, Bunbun, Cinderella 新姫
Export Label(s)	Wakamusume, Cinderella
Homepage	https://wakamusume.com/
Tours	not offered; there is a direct-sales shop nearby

Shintani Shuzo is the smallest sake brewery in Yamaguchi in terms of both production and actual physical space. It has one fermentation room and two staff members and produces only 80 koku of sake despite brewing year-round. It is run completely by a husband and wife team, with husband Yoshinao running the business side and wife Fumiko in charge of brewing. With only the two of them, there is a lot of overlap in labor, but Fumiko is clear on one thing. "I am in charge of the sake recipe and koji making, and my husband listens when I am in the brewery."

Shintani is an excellent illustration of the turbulent history that has such resonance in the local sake brewing industry. For most of its history, it was a small but solid business making local sake for local fans. It was never a major producer but never seemed to be a failing one.

Yoshinao was born into that stable but moderate level of success, and business seemed set to continue until, of course, it could

not. Just when he had set out on his career and started his own family, the aging toji announced suddenly that he could not continue working because of health issues. Having to quickly replace an experienced toji was itself a serious issue for a small sake brewery, but the problem was compounded when the entire brewery staff decided to leave with him.

That left Yoshinao with a choice: Close the brewery, or start doing everything by himself. He chose the immensely difficult second option. In 2005, with a new wife and an infant daughter, Yoshinao started brewing on his own. He had not been trained as a toji, though he had helped out around the brewery when he was young. He took a short course from the National Research Institute of Brewing and then leapt in. He was only brewing a single tank at a time, with occasional help from his wife. She, though, was a nurse and mother of an infant, so the challenges were enormous.

But he persevered, and as he did Fumiko found herself more and more involved. "I couldn't just watch him do it all alone. He was working so hard to keep his family business afloat." As she took more time to help out in the brewery, something about the work took hold of her.

The brewery did achieve stability, eventually, and for a good ten years the family was able to keep its head above water. Fumiko not only helped out with brewing but also did sales work in the cities. Little by little, things began to look up. The first crisis seemed to be behind them.

"We were growing, bit by bit, so the fear let up. We even took out a loan to refit our old kura building for temperature-controlled cold brewing," Fumiko says. "Then, the roof collapsed. It was a nightmare. We had just installed the cooling equipment and had a loan out already. That was actually the closest we ever came to closing down, even closer than the first crisis."

Even if they found the resources to rebuild, the pair realized that their current arrangement simply would not work with the added burden of more loans. That was when Fumiko decided to quit her job as a nurse to work full time in the brewery. Balancing two jobs was stressful, and the family brewery was simply too important to ignore. But, if she was going to do the work, she wanted to make sake her way. She would become toji.

"I studied under some experts and got help from other local breweries," she says. "And from 2018, I was the toji. I told myself that I would give it three years, and if it didn't seem to be working then, I'd quit."

The Shintanis built a new kura inside a warehouse on their property, with two new koji rooms at Fumiko's request. The dynamics of this struck me as potentially difficult, since Yoshinao had been the toji of his own brewery for ten years, but Fumiko says it has gone smoothly. "I decided everything for the new kura, and my husband just agreed. He hasn't resisted handing over the brewing. We fight, like any couple, but not over that."

It would appear that Yoshinao made a wise choice, because since Fumiko took over as toji the Wakamusume label has found amazing success, despite yet a *third* crisis.

"It's almost hard to believe. Just after we got the new kura up and running in 2019, 2020 came and brought the pandemic." Sake's primary domestic market is through restaurants and related businesses, especially in the big cities, and Covid essentially killed all of that business. "We had months in early 2020 with hardly any sales. It was terrifying." They stopped brewing because they had no place left to store sake.

The turning point came in June 2020, Fumiko says. "The Annual Japan Sake awards were announced. There were no gold medals awarded in 2020, but we got silver and it was the first time we ever even entered." The announcement made people take notice, and media attention immediately translated into sales. "All of the stock that was backed up from those months of low sales disappeared completely in July, and then people kept asking for more." The pair restarted brewing as fast as they could. Demand surged even higher after they won gold at the Hiroshima Regional Sake Awards in August, but the biggest spike came in October.

"Winning platinum at the KuraMaster awards in Paris was almost more than I could believe," Shintani says. The tiny brewery was featured as one of the top five junmai daiginjo in the competition, putting it on the world stage with famous brands like Zaku. "It was like a dream. We were getting interview requests from TV stations and newspapers, and as word spread online, people were seeing it all over Japan." They began fielding orders from private customers both new and old with such regularity that they opened an online store—but they are usually unable to keep enough sake in stock to cover orders for more than a few days a month. Demand has only continued to grow, especially with the brewery finally winning the coveted Annual Japan Sake Award Gold in 2021.

The Shintanis were struggling to increase production even as we spoke before that win, in early 2021. "We bought two more fermentation tanks, but with only the two of us, we haven't been able to use them." Their current production of 80 koku is more than 150% of the 50 koku they were making before the pandemic, and stock still sells out almost as soon as it is bottled.

So, I ask, how about the three-year limit she gave herself?

"I think this is the sign I was looking for. It has worked out," she says, "but it was very scary. And not just for us. I'm a member of the Kurajosei Summit, and we were always talking about what we could do to survive." The Kurajosei Summit is an organization of women in the sake industry that was established to offer mutual support in dealing with what is still very much a male-dominated industry. "Everyone has been really supportive of each other, especially during the pandemic. We have all talked about how to use online avenues to connect with customers and such," Fumiko says.

Shintani Shuzo has dodged disaster time after time and come back stronger than ever. Fumiko is quick to talk how much support the couple has received, both from some local brewers and her own colleagues in the Kurajosei Summit. But there has also been resistance. "When I was first starting out, I really didn't know how to do the work. I never went to formal training. I just learned watching my husband, and from talking to people in Tokyo during sales calls. So, when I took over as toji, a lot of people took it like I was pretending, or that my husband was actually the one doing the work. That was really hard. But now, I think people are convinced." It would take a hard head indeed to not be. . . .

(I am happy to note that a brewing helper was hired in the summer of 2022, after the main portion of this book was written.)

TOJI'S CHOICE SAKE

Wakamusume Kakitsubata Junmai Daiginjo
Seimaibuai: 40%
Rice: Saito no Shizuku

Wakamusume Kakitsubata is the label that won Platinum at the 2020 KuraMaster awards, as well as a regional trophy at the 2021 International Wine Challenge, and it is the first sake Shintani Shuzo ever submitted to the Annual Japan Sake Awards. It won silver the first time, in 2020 when there were no golds awarded, and then took gold the next time in 2021. The awards list goes on. As such, it represents for toji Shintani Fumiko validation of her decision to brew sake in the first place. It is also, as you might expect, excellent.

This sake presents complex, deep aromas with herbal, floral notes and a hint of melon and mochi rice sweetness. The flavors are big and bold, with a deep rounded sweetness. There are taste notes of melon, cherry, anise, and a reserved acidity that offers lovely balance. It is exceptionally satisfying and rewards slow sipping, without weighing down the palate for session drinking.

This kind of daiginjo makes one sit up and take notice and is truly astonishing coming from a toji who has been in charge of brewing for only a handful of years.

Yamashiroya Shuzo*

山城屋酒造

*Founded 1611**/1916*

Kuramoto	Miyazaki Tomoka
Toji	none
Production	NA
Main Label(s)	Sugihime 杉姫, Kojo no Homare 鴻城乃誉, Princess
Export Label(s)	NA
Homepage	https://sugihime.jp
Tours	not offered; there is a sake shop where the kura used to be

Yamashiroya Shuzo, maker of Sugihime sake, does not exist. Or rather, it exists on paper but not on the ground. Thus, the first asterisk on the name above. It is an example of the many, many "dormant" sake breweries that fill the tax office's ledgers, also known as "ghost kura." They do not actually brew their own sake, but they have the permission to do so—and to keep that permission, they must sell sake. It all comes down to licensing, one of the key issues to understanding some of the mysteries of sake brewing in Japan.

Once bestowed, the permission to brew sake is a treasure. The Japanese government has made getting an entirely new brewing license a near impossibility, so anyone who wants to become a sake brewer has little choice but to buy an existing license from a brewing family. And once a license exists, it is essentially eternal, with a few conditions. This is how, for example, old breweries like Kenbishi can claim five centuries of history—that's not the age of a building, or even a location, it is the age of a license. One of the conditions for

maintaining a brewing license through the years is selling a certain amount of sake under the label registered on the license. Note that wording: selling, not making.

So, a sake brewer can lose all its staff, and even its location, but contract with another brewer to make a certain amount of sake to order, label the bottles with their own label, and put it up for sale—all to keep that precious license active. The practice is incredibly common (Yamaguchi has about forty sake brewers on paper, but only twenty-three actively brewing sake today) and not really deceptive, since by law the label must show where the sake was brewed. It is a way to maintain a link to the past and a valuable business asset—and it keeps older generations of local fans happy.

And so, we come to Yamashiroya and the double asterisks on the founding date above. Yamashiroya has been a company since 1916. However, they possess a license that was granted in 1611—an early-Edo license! The story goes that the local Ouchi lords had retainers, the Abe family, who had permission to brew sake, and make miso and soy sauce, at their mountain castle (*yamashiro* in Japanese—get it?). At some point, no one is sure when, the Abes stopped brewing and passed the license to the Miyazaki family, who eventually founded an official brewing company in 1916. So, the license goes far, far back, but the company is much younger.

Even if the brewery itself is gone, the care and the attention to detail are there, and indeed the spirit of brewing is taking root once more in the Miyazaki family. Japan's dormant sake breweries are not dead—they can come back, as has happened with many others in Yamaguchi.

The issues that wracked the entire industry in World War II put an end to the company's sake-brewing business. Yamashiroya Shuzo went dormant, the business shifted to liquor sales, and current owner Miyazaki Tomoka's grandfather turned the land into a parking lot. But the current generation decided to turn things around. Tomoka's younger brother took over the sake brand and was working to revive the brewery when he suddenly passed away. Tomoka, who was running the real-estate branch of the family company, determined she wanted to keep her brother's dream alive and assumed the work he was doing.

Of course, Tomoka was not a sake brewer. She was a business manager. So, at first, she left everything to her subcontractor—Yamagata Honten in Shunan (see p. 89). It was when she attended her first sake event that she realized how little she knew about her own product and how important sake is to its fans, and she decided to take a more direct hand. She started learning about the process and went to meet rice farmers to learn about the best rice and rice fields.

Today Yamashiroya buys its own rice for their outsourced production from contract farmers in Yamaguchi City's Tokusa district, and even has tanker trucks bring the water from their well—sourced from one of Yamaguchi's most famous springs—for brewing at Yamagata Honten. Tomoka meets with the toji there to discuss variations and has even tried her hand at the brewing process. The ideas for the three labels they now make were all hers. Princess is a lighter, more fruity sake that she thinks will appeal to women. Kojo no Homare is drier, and heavier. Tomoka intended it for men—but the actual responses have been quite the opposite, she says, with many women being very vocal about their love of the latter and many men coming to buy the former. She laughs when she talks about this and admits she still has a lot to learn about sake and its drinkers.

Tomoka does not claim to be a brewer and has no intention of ever taking up the toji mantle, but she respects the product and the process and has hopes that her own son might have enough interest to become the toji she knows she is not. Still in his teens, the boy has expressed an interest in the sake business, and so the hope remains alive.

All of this is why I think Yamashiroya deserves mention here. Even if the brewery itself is gone, the care and the attention to detail are there, and indeed the spirit of brewing is taking root once more in the Miyazaki family. Japan's dormant sake breweries are not dead—they can come back, as has happened with many others in Yamaguchi. It is exactly this kind of spirit that brought those breweries back, and I see no reason to think the same cannot happen for Yamashiroya.

connections

Doburoku and the Roots of Sake

The modern, legal term for what we are calling sake in this book is *seishu*, which is often defined as "refined alcohol." This term stands in opposition to the original roots of sake, which was decidedly unrefined. In the earliest days of Japan's drinking history, back when the imperial court at Nara was setting up a special department of brewing, commoners all over Japan were turning excess rice into a rough mash of rice, koji, water, and yeast—doburoku.

The word "doburoku" has come to mean something like "moonshine" in English. It refers to rough, unrefined booze, something for unsophisticated drinkers. That hearkens back to the fact that, even as sake brewing was being refined by the elites of the imperial court, rice was also being turned into hooch in countryside farm sheds, and the farmers did not feel the need to filter anything.

They just wanted their booze.

Today, doburoku—also called *dakushu*, using the same kanji characters—is a relative rarity on most shop shelves, though it is growing less so. Sake brewing requires a license, even for doburoku, and since there is such a small market for less-refined drinks the breweries that have such a license do not go out of their way to produce it.

There are, however, some who value doburoku for itself and for its place in the history and culture of sake in Japan. One of these is Migita Keiji, a founding member of Japan's Sake Service Institute and current head of the Japan Traditional Nigori Sake Research Institute. Migita has spent decades working to popularize sake and improve its reputation worldwide, but in later years has felt the need to go back to basics, as it were. He returned to his home in Yamaguchi and led the push to apply for Hofu's designation as a Special Doburoku District, which was granted in 2019.

This means that the Japanese government has given rice farmers with B&Bs or restaurants in the area special permission to use their own rice to make doburoku for personal consumption and small-scale sale at their own facilities. There are quite a few of these districts scattered around Japan, including two others in Yamaguchi, but few have the kind of dedicated brewing facilities that Migita has set up.

"I spent so many years on the outside, selling the idea of sake," he says. "I felt like it was time to get in the game myself." He chose doburoku not only because its path is more open than sake's, but also because he feels it has intrinsic value that needs recognition. "Doburoku is the heart of sake. It's pure, it's natural, and it's healthy. Modern sake is a fake, with the added alcohol and things. I spent years selling the fake stuff, but now I want to get at the truth." That truth, apparently, is doburoku.

The facilities he set up in the back of his house are about as small scale as they can be. A short hallway holds a small freezer, a rack of beakers for measuring alcohol content, and a blender. That hallway opens onto another that has three small pots of around four liters each to hold the moromi. Yet another hallway has a small kitchen-sized rice steamer and another freezer. The total space is somewhere between a large closet and a very small room, and of course output is not measured in the typical koku but in liters. "I'm not really sure how much we make, but it's not much. We sell out at the café every week." The café, Mizunoha, is key to his brewing permission. "To get a doburoku license, even in a special district, you have to be a rice farmer, and you have to have a restaurant or business that serves it. So, I bought some fields and opened a café." His wife runs the café, serving fresh-made ice cream, desserts, homemade curry, and of course doburoku.

"We have daily regulars. The main groups are old men like me, and young women." Perhaps those are the people most interested in the purported healthiness of the drink. "This stuff used to be a family drink, and everyone from small children to the sickest old people drank it. It heals you. It's not like these modern drinks that make you sick with all the sugar and everything. It's full of amino acids and natural sweetness. This is the real 'drinkable IV'!" He refers here to a common epithet for *amazake*, an alcohol-free drink made from sake lees or koji and water that many people drink for the supposed health benefits of the amino acids koji produces.

"We sell out every week, and people come asking me when more is coming. But it's just me and three other old guys. Well, two and a half. One just cleans and hauls water!" he laughs. He is teaching as many people how to make the drink as want to learn, though. "I think I've taught sixty or so people. I want there to be more, I want everyone to be able to drink it. But so far, no one else is brewing yet." More than just a drink, doburoku is an important part of Japanese culture, Migita says. "This is where Japanese sake started: made at home, by farmers, for their families and neighbors. It's pure Japanese culture. Then the government went and made it illegal, and we lost that culture. I guess someone realized that was a problem, so they started this special-district program, but it was lost for so long that it's taking time to bring it back."

The fact that so many local people keep coming back for more indicates there is certainly room in modern life for this ancient drink to make a resurgence.

Takeuchi Shuzojo
竹内酒造場

Founded 1909

Kuramoto	Takeuchi Atsuko
Toji	Takeuchi Shigeo
Production	150 koku / 27 kiloliters
Main Label(s)	Nishikisekai 錦世界, Suobijin 周防美人
Export Label(s)	NA
Homepage	https://peraichi.com/landing_pages/view/takeuchishuzou/
Tours	not offered; may offer after current renovations

Takeuchi Shuzo is the only sake brewery in Hofu City, and that seems to have worked in its favor. The brewery is quite small, and until 2020 a hundred percent of its production was sold within the city limits (barring the odd order from people who stumble upon their new website). It is wholly family run. Takeuchi Atsuko is the current kuramoto; her son Takeuchi Shigeo took over as the current toji in 2019 after his father passed and does almost all the brewing himself. The toji's older brother is in charge of sales (as well as helping out with the brewing), and there is one office clerk. That is the totality of the staff.

The brewery building is a traditional wooden warehouse-style structure, with bare wooden beams holding up the rafters, and an ancient koji room with cedar-lined walls packed with rice husks to control humidity. "This room is really old and kind of musty, but that's part of the key to our sake," says Takeuchi toji. "We don't do

a lot of high-end ginjo-style brewing, which is all about aiming for a target flavor. Most of what we brew is lower level and has lots of natural expression. We use yeast from the Yamaguchi agricultural center, but it always mixes with the natural yeast in the kura. The koji is the same way. That old *kojimuro* is filled with its own spores, and they mix with the seed koji we spread." He says that this kind of brewing leads to unpredictability and instability, but for him that is part of what makes sake interesting. "Natural influence leads to complexity. Some people call it *zatsumi* [off flavors], but sometimes that's what sake needs," Takeuchi explains.

When I was there, the brewery staff were rearranging the layout and removing old tanks to make room for new ones and cooling equipment. "I'm not a fan myself, but sake shops keep asking for more ginjo-class sake. The kura is too old to install proper tank cooling equipment, so we have to use water-cooled tank wraps." Takeuchi does already produce two ginjo sake, however. One is made from Yamada Nishiki rice and the other from a Yamaguchi heirloom variety, Kokuryomiyako. The latter dates back to 1890, when a local agriculture expert selectively bred it from a wild variety; it is also a precursor strain to Yamaguchi's other, more popular sake rice, Saito no Shizuku. Very few breweries now use Kokuryomiyako, making this ginjo a rarity.

For someone who says he is not a ginjo fan, the toji certainly has not taken any shortcuts in attempting the style. He uses a rare rice, in a brewery unequipped for slow, cold ginjo brewing and without any previous experience making it. In fact, the only reason he even tries, he says, is because a "ghost kura" (a brewery that no longer brews their own sake but buys from others to relabel and sell to maintain its valuable brewing license) provides the highly polished rice for sale under its own label. The agreement allows Takeuchi to use some of that rice for its own purposes as well. This sake's quality is up to the high standards associated with the ginjo name, of course, but the brewing team all agree that their sake made from less-polished rice is where Takeuchi's production really shines.

> As a diehard futsushu fan, this is the stuff I love. A brewer who drinks their own futsushu is a brewer who truly understands the hearts of their long-time customers. This is a clean, rich, and full-bodied sake that leaves out added glucose in favor of an extra round of rice added late in the fermentation to bring natural sweetness.

That could be because the brewery is very much focused on rice. Takeuchi uses only rice grown in Yamaguchi, much of it from within the city limits. Sub-label Suobijin is brewed from Hofu rice, milled at a local table-rice processor to only 90% seimaibuai. The resulting rich, dry sake is like a reincarnation of something from another age, filled with complexity and weight that can only come from allowing the koji and yeast to ferment away with a full touch of nature's influence. "The rice is barely milled in this, but I think it's good. Don't you?" the toji asks, and I can only nod. I do.

I think the same of their futsushu, which they brew from locally grown Nihonbare rice milled to 90% in a four-stage brewing process (most sake is brewed in a three-stage process, called *sandan jikomi*). "This is what I drink," Takeuchi says. "Futsushu should be sweet, but it should finish quickly. It's a meal drink, so it should help food come through without getting in the way. Those ginjo aromas are distracting when you're trying to eat." As a diehard futsushu fan, this is the stuff I love. A brewer who drinks their own futsushu is a brewer who truly understands the hearts of their long-time customers. This is a clean, rich, and full-bodied sake that leaves out added glucose in favor of an extra round of rice added late in the fermentation to bring natural sweetness.

"The priests at Hofu Tenmangu use this for their *omiki*," he adds. Hofu Tenmangu is the city's oldest, and largest, Shinto shrine and the oldest of the twelve thousand or so Tenmangu shrines in Japan, dating back to 904; *omiki* is the sake used in sacred Shinto rituals. This connection is immensely important to the toji. "They gave us this woodblock design of the main shrine hall so we could put it on the labels," he says with obvious pride.

A sake brewery taking pride in futsushu is such a refreshing thing, and it results in a cheap, dependable sake that is always worth a try. That is exactly the kind of sake that demonstrates how it has organically grown as a fundamental element of the local food culture. If someone is truly interested in sake regionality and in local production for local consumption, I offer up Takeuchi Shuzo's humble Nishikisekai futsushu as a shining example of both.

TOJI'S CHOICE SAKE

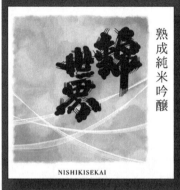

熟成純米吟醸

NISHIKISEKAI

Nishikisekai Junmai Ginjo
Seimaibuai: 60%
Rice: Kokuryomiyako

Nishikisekai Junmai Ginjo is one of only two ginjo-class sake that Takeuchi makes. The other uses Yamada Nishiki, but the staff all agreed on recommending this version, because the rice is a Yamaguchi Prefecture original. Kokuryomiyako was selectively bred in 1890 by local farmer Ito Otoichi (1856–1912). The rice soon became known for its large grains and low protein content, making it particularly well suited to brewing dry sake. It was difficult to grow, though, and fell out of favor not long after World War II. The rice was revived in the 1980s, and now a few local breweries use it for specialbrews. Takeuchi uses this rice because the brewery wants to be a part of preserving that tradition.

Ginjo brewing is a tricky affair, and Takeuchi brews very little at this premium level. When it does, it brings the same focus on complex, deep flavor as it does to its lower levels of brewing. The result is a distinctive take on junmai ginjo.

My bottle of this ginjo had aged for two years, bringing a deeper, rounder level of umami than would be found in a younger sake. But its most prominent characteristic is a robust acidity that makes it distinctly meal-oriented. It pairs well with heavy, oily meat and robustly flavored dishes. This is intended, like all of Takeuchi's brews, to be a table sake. It is rare to encounter a ginjo sake with this kind of complex, challenging profile.

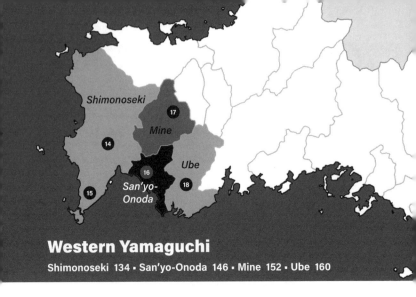

Western Yamaguchi

Shimonoseki 134 · San'yo-Onoda 146 · Mine 152 · Ube 160

SHIMONOSEKI (population 251,904 as of 2022) is the largest city in Yamaguchi Prefecture and plays a dominating role in many facets of life here. It is a tourist hub, a financial center, and the gateway to Kyushu Island. Its location at the very tip of Honshu means it has long dominated the Kanmon Straits between it and Kyushu, with enormous military and financial implications.

Many of the major incidents in Shimonoseki's history have been military in nature. The Battle of Dan-no-ura in 1185, which marked the end of the Genpei War, took place in the Kanmon Straits just off of Shimonoseki. Here the Minamoto (Genji) clan defeated their enemies, the Taira (or Heike) clan, many of whom lost their lives—including the child emperor Antoku. Legends say that the souls of the dead linger on in the Heike crabs of Kanmon, which supposedly bear the scowling faces of defeated samurai on their shells.

Shimonoseki was also the location of legendary swordsman Miyamoto Musashi's duel with Sasaki Kojiro on tiny Ganryu-jima island. There are monuments to this famous battle on the island, which can be reached by ferry from Shimonoseki port.

Shimonoseki is also one of the first places that the United States and Japan came into direct military conflict. The Mori clan took the imperial order to expel foreigners from Japan very seriously and began shelling every foreign ship passing through the narrow Kanmon Straits. In 1863 the United States Navy ship *USS Wyoming* retaliated by attacking the Japanese fleet in Shimonoseki and sinking two ships. The conflict did not end there and led to a full-on campaign against the city that extended into 1864.

In 1871, China signed the Treaty of Shimonoseki, ceding defeat to Imperial Japanese Army forces in the First Sino-Japanese War and granting Japan control over Taiwan, Dalian, and Penghu. Attending the treaty signing in the city were the Chinese emperor, American diplomats, and numerous Japanese dignitaries, including the future first prime minister of Japan, Ito Hirobumi.

A place with such importance, with such connections, would seem to call for more sake breweries than it has now. Of course, it did have more, once. A 1958 chart of sake breweries shows it having six, which even then was a small number. One possible explanation of this is that, because Shimonoseki is essentially a peninsula, there is little farmland and lots of shipping, so there was less need and less supply for local sake brewing.

Whatever the reason, this large city now only has two operating sake breweries. Shimonoseki Shuzo is an urban brewery, found amidst the winding city roads, while Choshu Shuzo is in outlying farmland in the Kikugawa area.

SAN'YO-ONODA (population 60,302 as of 2020) is a small industrial city at the western end of Yamaguchi. It was built out of many small communities during Japan's period of municipal conglomeration in the early 2000s, and one of those communities absorbed was the small town of Asa. San'yo-Onoda's lone sake brewery, Nagayama Shuzo, still calls itself an Asa brewery.

The economy is largely dominated by manufacturing, with a cement plant propping up the local economy. Given the city's relatively small size, the outlying areas are still blessed with scenic coastline and beautiful mountains, and the general lack of urbanization means that the water and land remain relatively clean. Even beyond sake, it's a place whose countryside is worth exploring. Nagayama Shuzo takes advantage of this environment in one unexpected way: It also runs Yamaguchi's sole winery!

MINE—pronounced *mii-neh*—(population 23,247 as of 2020) is a small town in the rolling foothills at the tail end of the Chugoku mountain range. It is more farmland than town, in fact, and is home to some of the most beautiful scenery in the prefecture. It lays claim to Yamaguchi's famous karst-dotted Akiyoshidai Plateau, and the countryside is full of caves, springs, and places to explore.

This area is also one of Yamaguchi's oldest settled spots. The many hollows on the plateau gathered water and offered excellent gardening spots for paleolithic Jomon villages, while the ancient forests were prime hunting grounds. Later, with the coming of Yayoi agriculture, the forests were cleared and planted with pampas grass for pastureland or were converted to rice fields. The annual burning of the pampas grass, a custom that continues to this day at Akiyoshidai, has kept the forests from regrowing.

Rainfall on the plateau filters through limestone and granite to feed into streams and springs that have made the area quite well known locally for clean water, some of which finds its way to distant breweries like Nagayama Honke Shuzojo in Ube city. The streams have also carved out several caves in the area, including

Japan's longest limestone cavern, Akiyoshido. One of the other springs feeds Beppu Benten Ike, a crystalline blue pond in the middle of a quiet pine forest, which runs out into a small stream that provides clean, soft brewing water for Ohmine Shuzo, the area's only sake brewery.

UBE (population 160,838 as of 2022) is highly urbanized and largely dominated by the chemical factories of multinational Ube Industries, along with several other manufacturing concerns like Central Glass and Renesas. These companies keep the local economy robust but leave much to be desired in the pristine natural scenery department.

Ube's history is not particularly illustrious. It began as a coal-mining village and owes its growth to the expansion of undersea mining operations in the Meiji period. As a result, it lacks many of the historical buildings, ruins, and castles of other notable cities in Yamaguchi. It does have Sorin-ji, a small Zen temple with a beautiful garden named Ryushintei. Sadly, Ube's primary source of interest to the traveler will likely be its airport, with multiple flights to and from Tokyo daily.

The financial contributions from the factories help support some worthy initiatives, however. The government actively seeks out young artists from all over the world to put up statues and art installations all over the city. There is a particularly large concentration of pieces at sweeping Tokiwa Park on the south side of town, which is also home to the Ube Biennale, a biannual outdoor sculpture competition held here since 1961. The park also has a small zoo and botanical garden.

The urbanized center quickly gives way to rolling countryside. Ube's outlying areas still have clean rivers and wide-open rice fields, which local sake superstar Nagayama Honke Shuzojo, home of the immensely popular Taka brand, puts to fantastic use.

Choshu Shuzo
長州酒造

Founded 2019/1879*

Kuramoto	Okamoto Susumu
Toji	Fujioka Miki
Production	not disclosed
Main Label(s)	Tenbi 天美
Export Label(s)	none
Homepage	https://choshusake.com
Tours	not offered; the brewery has a cafe with tasting and a second-floor area with a view of the brewing facilities, interactive displays, and a sake-brewing library

Choshu Shuzo is the newest sake brewery in Yamaguchi in every meaningful sense—except the brewing license from the government. Its riverside location in the Kikugawa district of rural Shimonoseki, blessed by clean water and rolling rice fields, has in fact been home to a sake brewery for over a hundred and forty years. Kodama Shuzo stopped brewing there around 2005, when its toji grew too old to do the work, but had been able to retain its license by outsourcing its Kikugawa label to another producer. The buildings remained, though, built around a well of clean, soft water.

That water is the key to the brewery's rebirth as Choshu Shuzo. A few years ago, Okamoto Susumu—CEO of local solar-power-equipment manufacturer Choshu Industry—had an idea for a new venture: raising sturgeon for caviar production. In searching for a source of good water for sturgeon breeding, he encountered

Kodama Shuzo and its well just when it was on the brink of closing altogether. The idea of losing this part of local history struck Okamoto as terribly sad, so in 2017 he purchased the brewery lock, stock, and barrel. Of course, Okamoto was no sake brewer, and the facilities were old and out of use. So he decided to start from scratch. He tore down the old buildings and built everything anew. All new staff were hired. An acquaintance recommended Fujioka Miki to take over as toji, and after some initial hesitation, she agreed.

Fujioka is from Mie Prefecture, and her career includes stints at breweries in Nara, Kagawa, and eventually at Mie powerhouse Zaku. She had fallen in love with sake brewing when studying microbiology at Tokyo University of Agriculture and had been on the toji track since graduation. "Once I realized how serious President Okamoto was, I couldn't say no. It's such an incredible opportunity to help set up your own sake brewery from scratch. I helped design it from the ground up." The brewery is housed in totally new facilities, but Kodama Shuzo has not been completely lost. "We couldn't let the history that was built here disappear. When we took over the license, I met with the family that had owned Kodama. The old kuramoto's sister asked me to protect her family legacy with tears in her eyes, and I promised I would." Part of that legacy is going to be the eventual revival of Kodama's old local label, Kikugawa, and the rest is in the fabric of the brewery itself.

"We used as much of the old brewery's materials as we could," Fujioka says, pointing out red bits of brick in the stucco of the new brewery's entryway. "The old bricks of the building were crushed and mixed into the stucco and mortar, and the beams were carved into stools or used in the doorframes." The old brewery's pot-style rice steamer, or *kama*, now sits in front of Choshu Shuzo as a reminder of the lineage that it carries.

But most of Choshu Shuzo is new, and the sake is a perfect example of that. When I wrote this in 2021, Choshu Shuzo was finishing its very first season of brewing new label Tenbi. The sake has since taken Japan by storm. It was a darling of sake social media from the very first release, Tenbi The First, and pop idol/sake expert Takano Yui even featured it on her YouTube channel. More than just buzz, though, it is very well-made sake. Tenbi won silver at the Annual Japan Sake Awards in its very first year, and its super-limited junmai daiginjo shizuku bottling has become the stuff of legend. Even the standard tokubetsu junmai can be hard to get without reserving a bottle in advance.

Which makes it ironic to look back at the first time I spoke with Fujioka, in March of 2020, before the brewery had even had its first shipment of rice. "I was so nervous about coming to Yamaguchi," she said. "There are so many great sake breweries here that I thought the competition would be so strict." She said, however, that everyone has been very welcoming. "I actually went to university with Nagayama Takahiro [of Nagayama Honke Shuzojo/Taka fame] so that helped ease my nerves." Now that the sake is out and has gained such success, it is doubtful those nerves remain.

That is not to say that getting from there to here was easy. Brewing was scheduled to begin in June of 2020, but delay after delay pushed it back to November. There were issues with residual aromas from the brand-new equipment, and Fujioka's social media was packed with pictures of staff washing it time and again. Then, the water source had trouble. "It seems like leaving a well unused for fifteen years takes longer to get past than predicted," one of her posts reads.

What about the future, which is where Choshu Shuzo must be looking? "The sake I want to make is modern, of course, and I want it to be something young people enjoy," Fujioka said, "but most of all I want to build and maintain the local connections. A sake brewery is always rooted in the local community and culture, and I don't want that to change." Choshu Shuzo is going to expand its use of local rice, she said, and by doing that help support local farming.

Another way that Choshu Shuzo hopes to shore up the local district is through tourism. "One of the things I planned into the design is to allow for tours to come in without getting in the way of production," Fujioka explains as she takes me up to the second floor of the brewery. From there, a winding hallway lined with huge windows allows a view of everything that happens on the brewing floor. "We haven't worked out the details yet, but we want to bring sakagura tourism to Kikugawa someday." This foresight is exciting, to say the least. No other brewery in Yamaguchi is so well prepared to welcome tourism, not even major players like Dassai or Toyobijin. With the Tenbi label's massive reputation, there is little doubt that Choshu will be able to draw visitors when the time comes.

"But before all of that," Fujioka says, "is the sake. It has to stand for itself. All the branding and the tourism is secondary. The sake comes first."

TOJI'S CHOICE SAKE

Tenbi Junmai Ginjo (Tenbi White)
Seimaibuai: 60%
Rice: Yamada Nishiki

This book was written right as Choshu Shuzo was in its first brewing season, so the brewery had yet to establish a solid style or reputation. Toji Fujioka Miki was an experienced brewer, so there was a solid foundation of skill there. But beginnings are tricky, and the first year was a tumultuous one for Choshu.

With that in mind, I waited until near the end of that first season to request a sake recommendation from Fujioka, so that she had had a chance to get a feel for the new equipment and climate she was working in. Her choice was Tenbi White.

Choshu Shuzo currently has two main production labels, distinguished by the color of the logo: white or black. Black is a tokubetsu junmai, and white is a junmai ginjo. The initial runs were all nama, but there are now pasteurized versions readily available (maybe not so "readily," given their extreme popularity). There are also super-premium daiginjo versions with a more sophisticated all-black label, including *fukurozuri*-pressed bottles that are rarer than hen's teeth.

With time, the color lineup has also grown to include Snow (*yuki* in Japanese) Tenbi, which is a cloudy nigori, as well as Pink (*momo*, or peach) Tenbi usunigori nama genshu—a lightly cloudy unpasteurized, undiluted version. These have grown just as popular as the core white and black labels, as any look at Japan's social media networks can attest.

The Tenbi Junmai Ginjo is the one Fujioka considers her core sake. "This is the sake that I want to make," she explained, "and the one I really want people to drink."

It opens up with rich, tropical-fruit aromas of ripe mango, lychee, and a hint of honey. The flavor is vibrant and fruity, as well. The first sip brings melon and juicy fruit notes, with assertive acidity to add a tart touch. It is all balanced around an umami core that keeps the structure together. The finish is quick and clean, with just a hint of umami lingering to encourage further drinking.

Fujioka's idea to create sake for a wider, particularly younger audience seems to have hit the nail on the head. This sake is a definite crowd pleaser, and I think that in times to come it will gain only more momentum.

Shimonoseki Shuzo 15
下関酒造

Founded 1923

President	Uchida Tadaomi
Leader	Murata Noboru
Production	1,200 koku / 216 kiloliters
Main Label(s)	Sekimusume 関娘, Kaikyo 海響, Kurabito no Jimansake 蔵人の自慢酒, Shido 獅道
Export Label(s)	Kurabito no Jimansake 蔵人の自慢酒, Shido 獅道, Kaikyo 海響
Homepage	https://www.shimonoseki.love/
Tours	not offered; there is a café and direct-sales shop on-site

Shimonoseki Shuzo is an urban sake brewery, located in a mixed residential/business district in Yamaguchi's largest city, Shimonoseki. Its facilities are relatively new, belying the age-stained brick smokestack that serves to mark it as you approach. The main production area was built in 1992; the café and sales area are housed in older parts of the facilities but only date back to the early 2000s.

Its relative youth is not the most unusual thing about this brewery. Eagle-eyed readers may have wondered about the missing titles "kuramoto" and "toji" at the head of this chapter. Larger corporate breweries don't often use such titles, but the overwhelming majority of breweries in this smaller size range almost always use the traditional terms. Shimonoseki Shuzo, however, was never a traditional family brewery. It was founded in 1923 by 445 local rice farmers who joined together to start a corporation to brew sake from

the rice they themselves had grown. The brewery is still incorporated as such, and the 92 stock owners are all descendants of original founders.

That means that the CEO/President is exactly that, rather than the head of the owner family. I spoke to Uchida Takanori, managing director and son of the current president, about this unusual organization. "The board elects a president who brings skills that the current management lacks. I'm on track to be the third generation of my family to be president, but that's not because we inherit the position. My grandfather was elected the fourth president because the third was a terrible salesman, and my grandfather was not. His sales skill brought the company success. My father, in turn, was very good with machines, and he was elected to modernize the equipment in the brewery," Uchida explains. When I ask about his own future, he says, "I've been getting ready to work for the brewery since I was ten years old. My father insisted I study something else and work outside the industry first. I studied architecture at university in Kobe and then worked in a different industry. Everything was to get ready to help the brewery, though. I even studied abroad in England for a year to learn English and get to know the market there, because I think the export market is the future."

Uchida has also overseen several other new developments. He spearheaded a new online shop, a redesign of the official website, and the brewery's café and restaurant. He is also the idea man behind the company's recent foray into premium sake, with two junmai daiginjo: Kurabito no Jiman Sake and Shido. His stated goal with these is to break into the foreign market, and they mark the first time the brewery has ever attempted junmai sake in the ginjo grade. He even went so far as to design the labels and packaging himself.

> The fact is that Shimonoseki Shuzo still has a lot of room to grow, in many senses. The brewing staff are all relatively young, and most came from other industries—there is still very little experience on the floor. They make up for their lack of experience with enthusiasm and sincerity about their work, and they are making huge strides in a short period. The management, as well, is already putting more in the hands of the younger Uchida, although many of his major initiatives are still not fully tested.

Young Takanori is bringing outside perspective, management skills, and export preparedness to the company, and his future seems secure now that the two new labels have begun winning awards internationally.

Production leader Murata Noboru also began his career outside the traditional brewing system. Up until around 2004 he was an engineer with a semiconductor manufacturer. Corporate restructuring forced him to look for another job, and his local sake brewery happened to be hiring. He has worked for Shimonoseki Shuzo ever since, becoming the production leader around 2016. Murata recognizes the tension of working on a premium-sake line with the relatively young team he leads. "I still feel like we lack some of the skills needed, but I do think our sake has gotten much better in the last few years." Since no one at the brewery had any experience at higher levels of brewing, Murata has depended on expert instruction from the prefectural technology center, which offers a range of technical advice and support to local sake brewers.

The sake Murata hopes to make, and that Takanori is pushing for, is dinner sake. "The goal for us is sake that is almost like water," Takanori says. "Not flavorless, or without character, but in the sense that it goes with any food. Water doesn't clash with any cuisine, it always works. That's what we want for our sake."

The brewery considers its different labels as geared to different cuisines. Sekimusume, for example, is the local label and is intended to pair with Shimonoseki's local home cuisine—especially blowfish, for which the city is famous all over Japan. This sake also serves as the basis for a true local specialty, *fukuhire* sake. *Fukuhire* means blowfish fin, and this sake is made by popping a dried blowfish fin into a rich, hot cup of futsushu; some izakaya in Shimonoseki even flambé the top. Shimonoseki Shuzo now offers the brew in a pre-finned one-cup package, as well as a more DIY version with a dried fin packaged with a bottle of Sekimusume.

Kaikyo is another local label and is intended for a wide variety of seafood. As such, it is designed to be fairly reserved to avoid excessive aroma or flavor so that it can meld seamlessly with all kinds of local dishes. The brewery's premium-sake labels, though, are geared for foreign cuisine with lots of herbs and fuller flavors, so they have more pronounced aromas and flavor profiles. "These are the sake we're entering in contests abroad," Takanori says. "We started out just to test our strength, but the results have been really great."

Much of this, however, is a look at the future. The fact is that Shimonoseki Shuzo still has a lot of room to grow, in many senses. The brewing staff are all relatively young, and most came from other industries—there is still very little experience on the floor. They make up for their lack of experience with enthusiasm and sincerity about their work, and they are making huge strides in a short period. The management, as well, is already putting more in the hands of the younger Uchida, although many of his major initiatives are still not fully tested. Murata is aware of the challenges and seems ready. "I'm not satisfied with our progress yet," he says. "But we're working hard."

BREWER'S CHOICE SAKE

we will never forget the spirit of the 445 founders

純米大吟醸 三割八分精米

Shido 38
Seimaibuai: 38%
Rice: Yamada Nishiki

Shido 38 is Shimonoseki Shuzo's pinnacle sake. The first junmai daiginjo they attempted, Kura-bito no Jimansake, comes in at a seimaibuai of 50%, but this one brings their production into the heady sub-40% range. Made from locally grown Yamada Nishiki rice, Shido 38 is intended to show that Shimonoseki Shuzo is ready to join the world as a premium-sake brand.

"When I came back to the brewery after working outside the industry for a few years," says Managing Director Uchida Takanori, "it was right around when our former production leader left. That meant our team was all fairly young and new. I thought it was the perfect time to try forging a new path."

This intent is what informed the name Shido, which roughly translates to "the lion's road." "The traditional path, the one that everyone follows and is considered the 'high road,' is the Odo—the king's road. But when you break out on your own and forge your own path, that's the lion's road. We are following the lion's road, with a young team making sake our own way," Takanori says. The striking label design is also a nod to that. The kanji for Shido—獅道—are stylized, written in an artistic calligraphy that recalls a lion's face.

In the glass, the sake first presents a full aroma of complex fruit and clean Yamada Nishiki sweetness, with notes of mango, cherry, and vanilla. The initial sip is big and airy, with those notes of vanilla, mochi, and melon striking first. The sweetness fades, though, into a finish that strikes hard. There are notes of tea-like astringency, a bit of bitterness, and a lingering off-note that seems to ask for food to help clear it away.

The sake has a clear initial expression of Yamada Nishiki junmai daiginjo character, and the aroma is quite well balanced. However, the finish still strikes as unbalanced, and speaks to the fact that the brewers are still finding their way with the premium-sake grades. That is understandable given that the brewery has only been working with these levels for a few years, and the effort gives me a lot of hope for the future of this unique Yamaguchi brewery.

Nagayama Shuzo
永山酒造

Founded 1887

Kuramoto	Nagayama Junichiro
Toji	Nagayama Gentaro
Production	400 koku / 72 kiloliters
Main Label(s)	Yamazaru 山猿, Otokoyama 男山
Export Label(s)	Yamazaru
Homepage	https://www.yamanosake.com/
Tours	available with reservations; no English support on-site

Nagayama Shuzo is located in the middle of the small community of Asa, which is technically part of San'yo-Onoda City in western Yamaguchi. Although near a shinkansen station, this is still a relatively hidden spot, and in many ways Nagayama Shuzo remains overshadowed by many other Yamaguchi breweries despite its powerful position in the prefecture's sake-brewing history. "We were the first brewery to release a junmai sake in Yamaguchi, and it saved us," says fifth-generation kuramoto Nagayama Jun'ichiro, whose son Gentaro became Yamaguchi's youngest toji at just twenty-eight years old.

"Back in the 1980s, my father was in charge, and he was thinking of giving it all up. Our sake wasn't selling. But I was ready to fix all that. I told him that I would go to university, and I would turn the business around," Jun'ichiro says. "I went to Tokyo University of Agriculture from 1982, and while I was there I would take time off to go visit all the big retailers in the city. My professors even

covered for me when they heard I was skipping classes for sales work."

This period was just after the floor had dropped out of the sake market, and the mass producers in Kyoto, Kobe, and Hiroshima had stopped buying on contract from other breweries. Consumer tastes had started to turn away from the big names, and the "local sake boom" was just kicking off. Urban sake lovers had found that the traditionally produced brews from small countryside makers offered higher quality and more interesting sake, often at lower prices. This is the world that Junichiro stumbled into.

"The first thing I learned was that Yamaguchi was odd. In other rural prefectures, local people drank local brands. Not us. Our local sake brewers had put all their work into making stuff on contract for major breweries, so there was hardly any local sake sold as such. Yamaguchi breweries would actually advertise the fact that their sake was being sold under other labels!"

But in the early '80s, all those sales had stopped, and since Yamaguchi had given up so much of its local sake brewing in favor of supplying other breweries, there was little chance to jump onto the local sake boom. "Tokyo retailers told me that we had to start making junmai. One gave me a bottle of Koshi no Kanbai [a Niigata brew that is often considered the very first local brand to sell purely on word of mouth] and said I should be making sake like that. I carried it home in my arms like a baby and drank it with our toji. I told him we needed to start making junmai, and he agreed to try. We put out a junmai sake in 1983 and started selling in Tokyo soon after. It was a top-five seller for our Tokyo retailers. It kept us alive!" Junichiro says.

The premium-sake boom, which took big names like Dassai and Toyobijin into the spotlight, was still years away. This first step by Nagayama Shuzo, though, helped inspire others. Junichiro remembers talking to his Yamaguchi colleagues about shifting production to meet the demand in bigger cities, and from the 1990s there was a clear push across the prefecture to do just that. The rest is history.

Although Nagayama has never reached the enormous successes of other big Yamaguchi names, it has maintained a solid local reputation, and there are fans of its Yamazaru label all over Japan.

After young Gentaro took over brewing in 2019, things evolved again. "I worked at a couple of other breweries, including Rihaku in Shimane, after I graduated from university," he says. "Then, our previous toji announced he was retiring, so I hurried back to get ready and take over." Soon, the labels underwent some redesign, and Gentaro decided to make some production changes. "Japanese cuisine, like lots of other cultural elements, is very seasonal. I decided to follow that lead and made a different sake for all four seasons. The spring is a fresh-pressed shinshu for drinking with the wild mountain herbs of spring dining, while the summer is a full-flavored sake to go with traditional summer dishes like grilled eel and such. The autumn is an aged yamahai sake ideal for umami-rich fall ingredients like mushrooms, and winter's is a rich, two-year matured sake perfect for drinking warmed with winter hotpots."

Aging sake is something that the brewery has also been very intent on. "We have always made sake for aging. Such sake should be less aromatic, and the yeast is very important," Gentaro says. The oldest sake Nagayama sells is over forty years old now, and interestingly it was aged at ambient temperature. "We have a brick warehouse full of tanks of old sake. Some of our newer matured brews are stored refrigerated, but for full aging we store in tanks without cooling to really bring out the depth that time creates." Many of Nagayama's aged sake offer big, rich koshu flavor and aroma at a relatively young age because of this warehouse storage method.

"I really want Yamazaru sake to show off how interesting it can be to follow the changes and developments that aging can bring," Gentaro says. "It's like making a time capsule of sake. I put aside some sake every year, and checking it every once in a while to see how it grows is wonderful."

Another aspect of Yamazaru sake is its focus on rich, *nojun* styles that take advantage of the water—Nagayama Shuzo's brewing water is the hardest in Yamaguchi. "It leads to very vigorous fermentation with lots of flavor, but we still always look for a clean finish." As a result, Gentaro says, Nagayama Shuzo tends to favor rice that is not the standard Yamada Nishiki. "The way we brew most of our sake, it would end up far too heavy with Yamada Nishiki. For the really full brews, we use Kokuryomiyako." This variety of rice was first grown in Yamaguchi in the 1890s and was often used in sake brewing until around World War II. It fell out of style until the 1990s, when Nagayama helped bring it back to local fields. The brewery released its first Kokuryomiyako sake in 2002 and with it inaugurated the Yamazaru label. "There are only a couple of breweries now using that rice, but I think we use the most."

Clearly, Nagayama Shuzo bucks the trends—it goes for rich, deep flavor rather than the delicate aromatic ginjo style that is all the rage, it uses rare heirloom rice when it could focus on Yamada Nishiki, and it embraces aging sake at a time when most in the industry still consider koshu a niche for nerds. Nagayama may not be the biggest name in Yamaguchi sake, but it is one well worth remembering.

It is also worth mentioning that Nagayama not only brews sake but also distills shochu, Japan's indigenous spirit, and has done so since the 1970s. The distillery is one of only two distilleries in Yamaguchi Prefecture and represents yet another way that Nagayama defies expectations. Its Netaro brand of rice shochu was conceived as a "truly Japanese brandy." It is distilled from a finished sake (though one made from waste rice and the rice powder left after milling its sake rice) just as brandy is distilled from wine. Nagayama also has a winery, and many of its Netaro expressions are aged in wine casks for even more complexity and drink synergy.

TOJI'S CHOICE SAKE

Nagayama Shuzo has gone through a bit of a change since young Nagayama Gentaro took over as toji, and one of the primary changes is an intense focus on yamahai styles. This traditional method of setting up a fermentation starter is particularly suited to the very hard water that Nagayama uses. "The fermentation is very vigorous," says Gentaro, "and we take advantage of that for thorough brewing to get the most flavor out of our sake." This means that the sake tends to be on the *nojun*, or rich, side, although Nagayama tries to keep that richness from weighing on the palate by bringing out a clean acidity to cut the finish off. That is one reason the brewery still uses the heirloom rice Kokuryomiyako.

"If we used Yamada Nishiki in these really rich brews, it would

山廃仕込

無濾過牛原酒

Yamazaru

**Yamazaru Yamahai Muroka
Nama Genshu**
Seimaibuai: 60%
Rice: Kokuryomiyako

get too heavy," Gentaro says. Yamada Nishiki dissolves very easily in ferments like this, which might pump too many amino acids into the finished sake. "For this, a harder rice like Kokuryomiyako meets our target better." This is why the brewery chose its Yamazaru Yamahai Muroka Nama Genshu to recommend here.

It is rare to see a nama yamahai, so I was interested right away. I felt this sake was going to offer something unique, and I was right.

Yamahai sake has a tendency toward complex, umami-rich flavors, and that is this one in a nutshell. The initial aroma offered notes of subtle sweetness, with vanilla and rice, There was also a strong savory note that reminded me of eggs—particularly a Japanese dish called *chawanmushi*, which is a steamed dish made from eggs and *dashi* stock, almost like a savory custard.

The flavors followed the aromas closely: big, complex, and savory. It was rich and delicious, but not at all overpowering on the tongue, just as the toji intended. It seems this is exactly the flavor that Nagayama is aiming for, and I think it's one worth pursuing.

Ohmine Shuzo
大嶺酒造

Founded 1822

Kuramoto	Akiyama Takeshi
Toji	not disclosed
Production	not disclosed
Main Label(s)	Ohmine
Export Label(s)	Ohmine
Homepage	http://www.ohmine.jp/
Tours	not offered; there is a café and sake-tasting and sales space on-site

Ohmine Shuzo is both the most public and open of the sake breweries in Yamaguchi and somehow the most secretive. It comprises a bright white box of a building holding a café and a big black box containing the brewing facility, looking less like a sake brewery than a modernist rice museum. Surrounded by rice fields and lumber plants, it sits amidst the beautiful scenery of rural Mine not far from the brilliantly blue spring-fed Beppu Benten pond, which supplies the brewery with its water, and it is not far from Yamaguchi's famous Akiyoshidai Plateau.

All of this means it is a lovely place to stop off and get a cup of coffee. The parking lot is full on weekends with locals coming to do that just that, or perhaps enjoy a bit of ice cream, or even—if a designated driver is available—a sake flight. Inside, staff dressed in chic black designer uniforms offer up pour-over coffee at big-city prices in a sparkling space filled with the sound of R&B hits.

The café space is adjacent to the brewing area, and generous windows allow for a good view of the brewing work, and you can even use the free Wi-Fi to post Instagram-worthy pics, as many people do. The staff is friendly and welcoming, but they are café staff, not brewers.

I have visited Ohmine a handful of times and encountered staff at sake events all over the prefecture. Yet I know no more about the inner workings now than I did the first time I went, back in 2018. The toji's name, for example, is not public, and my inquiries in person and by email about the details of Ohmine brewing were rebuffed. I cannot tell you much about their rice sourcing, the yeast, or essentially any other details of the operation. The brewery's position is, explicitly and implicitly, that the sake should speak for itself, without any influence of names or numbers.

So, what can I tell you?

Ohmine Shuzo was founded in the center of Mine village in 1822.

It went dormant in 1955, and the brewing license eventually passed to local architectural firm Akiyama Kensetsu. The current kuramoto, Akiyama Takeshi, is the son of that company's president, and in 2010 he decided to reopen the brewery on his own. In 2018 he moved it to its new, modern, stylish building and celebrated with a party featuring DJs mixing at turntables, supermodels, and BMX bikers.

This history is told inside the café by a neon sign just inside the door that reads:

1822   Born
1955   Dead
2010   Reborn
2018   Against Sake World

That says it all, really. Ohmine Shuzo has taken an outsider approach to the sake industry. It rejects many of the things that guide other sake makers. It does not advertise its product using classifications, specifications, or rice. Its focus is on style—bottle designs, model photoshoots, collaborations with international pop stars...

Yes, pop stars. Ohmine Shuzo has produced sake for a collaboration between Tokyo designer NIGO and Pharrell Williams, the singer, who actually visited the sleepy Mine countryside for photo shoots and a tour. One can only imagine the entourage stopping by a local udon shop for selfies over the tempura shrimp—one more surreal note for a brewery that is itself almost a portrait of the surreal.

After several rounds of back and forth with the company PR department, I was finally able to glean some very basic insights about the company and its methods. I was able to find out, for example, that Ohmine "builds on a traditional recipe and uses modern technology to create sake that previous generations could never have made." They look for "a delicate balance of umami, sweetness, and acidity." And they use "some sake rice from inside Yamaguchi, some from outside, and have all kinds of contracts."

Everything else I can say about Ohmine is what is already public, like the fact that all of their sake is in the junmai daiginjo class. That their label design, with its intuitive grading system of 3, 2, or 1 grains of rice (from least to most polished), has won international awards for global design powerhouse Stockholm Design Lab. And . . . that is it.

I wish I could talk to someone with more inside knowledge. Someone who could tell me why they built a new, modern facility in this specific place, so far afield from train stations, bus lines, or even highway on-ramps—a somewhat risky choice for a place serving alcohol. They could discuss why they chose to follow the super-premium daiginjo-only path. They could maybe even tell me all about how Ohmine Shuzo came to work with Pharrell Williams! These are things that would have been interesting to read about, I know. Alas.

In the end, if you are looking to learn about sake as a craft or a business, Ohmine Shuzo is perhaps not the best place to look for insight. If you would like to listen to Top 40 hits while you sip a pour-over coffee and watch people in designer uniforms make sake, this is your place. You can even buy a t-shirt to commemorate your visit.

AUTHOR'S CHOICE SAKE

Ohmine has long held back on providing advertising specifications on its sake. It prints the seimaibuai on its bottles but releases no information about yeasts, SMV, or other nerdy details. For several years, I was not even sure what kind of rice it was using—presumably Yamada Nishiki since everyone does. Now, though, some things seem to be changing, and the Ohmine 3-Grain bottle is an example.

Ohmine 3-Grain
Seimaibuai: 50%
Rice: Omachi

It prominently displays the Omachi name, and as a fan of that sake rice I was intrigued.

My past experiences with Ohmine have been hit and miss. I first tried the new brew in 2018, and it struck me as overly acidic and fruity, while not particularly deep or rich. Later efforts have come across as more varied. The winter-only Yuki Onna nigori was a delightfully sweet sake that killed at a party I held, while a flight of the standard 1-, 2-, and 3-grain brews at the café once again missed the mark with me. The sake in general tend toward the *tanrei*, or light, style, which can make sweet seem thin.

This bottle, however, was quite interesting and enjoyable. It brought round, smooth vanilla flavor with the fruit and rice, with a healthy touch of Omachi herbaceous notes. I noticed hints of anise and mint that matched well with the prominent apple notes. It was well balanced and full, while not overpowering with heavy sweetness.

Ohmine 3-Grain does not express the greater depth and complexity that I normally expect from an Omachi brew, but was honestly satisfying and enjoyable.

connections

Sake and Dining

If there is one bedrock fact about sake drinking in Japan, it is this: it involves food. Sake is a meal drink, or perhaps one could say that sake is considered a fundamental part of Japanese cuisine. There are, of course, exceptions. Dassai bills itself as a sake for slow sipping, and most brewers agree that super-aromatic daiginjo sake is less suitable for the dinner table, as its aromas interfere with Japan's delicately flavored dishes. But any time spent perusing brewery websites will offer up plenty of mentions of how well its sake goes with, or fails to clash with, food.

Nowhere in Yamaguchi is that idea explored more deeply than at Ube City's Sogo Shurui Tankyujo K (General Liquor Exploration Center K). This tiny restaurant seems so utterly alien to the quiet residential streets of Ube's Ajisu district that many walk by every day without ever knowing it is there. K occupies a single room in the owner's house outfitted with a small counter that seats a maximum of four people and is otherwise filled wall to wall and floor to ceiling with bottles. In that cozy space, chef/owner Matsushiro Kiichi serves chef's-choice meals of creative cuisine all made specifically to go with alcohol. And what alcohol there is . . .

K has a fine, even excellent, selection of wine and shochu, Japan's indigenous spirit, but it is the sake selection that shines. An industrial refrigerator packed with bottles is in the front, but it takes little work to convince Matsushiro to go to the mysterious "back room" to bring out even more rare delights. Matsushiro can source seemingly anything, even the rarest of sake. Nearly unobtainable national favorites like Juyondai, Jikon, Ibi, and Hanabi are nearly always on hand, and often there are bottles that cannot be had for any

Sogo Shurui Tankyujo K in Ube City

price. Matsushiro is able to do this because of his near obsessive focus on sake and the people who make it.

"Sake is a friend and a teacher," Matsushiro says. "It has so many things to teach about experience and connection to the world— the sky, the soil, the water, the air, the people, the soul." As such, everything about K, from the space to the food, is geared toward the enjoyment of sake. "It all starts with sake. Every dish for every meal is made to bring that much more enjoyment out of sake, from beginning to end." But Matsushiro also leaves room for the experience to grow on its own. "I don't try to force one way of enjoying it. I want to create a space where every guest can experience whatever drink is in front of them with greater interest and pleasure."

The food presented here is a

showcase of local flavors. "I consider myself lucky to be cooking in Yamaguchi. Yamaguchi is filled with outstanding produce, and I've been able to connect with truly conscientious producers so I can offer the absolute best of the best. The gratitude I feel for that is enormous." Matsushiro often presents a dish with a short explanation of not only what is in it but who grew the vegetables or caught the fish. The personal connection to the community and the food is an unshakable part of the experience here.

Those connections extend to the sake world. Matsushiro is able to stock rare labels like Ibi because of his personal friendships, both with brewers and sake retailers. The restaurant is reasonably near to Nagayama Honke Shuzojo, whose kuramoto/toji Nagayama Takahiro is a friend, so K is generously stocked with limited Taka editions. Matsushiro was one of the first to spot the rising star of Choshu Shuzo, making an early connection to toji Fujioka Miki. As a result, he was the only one who could serve me the coveted Tenbi Junmai Daiginjo Shizuku sake, of which only a few bottles ever existed. He even has hidden away in his stocks a bottle of the first sake brewed at Sumikawa Shuzo after it recovered from near obliteration in the flooding of 2013. And more treasures arrive every day.

"Yamaguchi's sake circle is so interesting," Matsushiro says. "We have everything from world-famous brands, to one of the newest breweries in the country. There are tiny breweries putting all their heart into making incredibly delicious sake, and breweries that died but have been reborn. There are so many stories, and so many unique breweries, it's almost hard to believe."

While he serves countless sake brands from outside Yamaguchi, Matsushiro—a Yamaguchi native born and bred—feels that the prefecture's sake has something truly special to offer. "With new brands like Tenbi, I think Yamaguchi sake is going to get even more attention, and nothing would make me happier than if Yamaguchi sake could bring a touch more happiness."

Nagayama Honke Shuzojo

永山本家酒造場

Founded 1888

Kuramoto	Nagayama Takahiro
Toji	Nagayama Takahiro
Production	1,200 koku / 216 kiloliters
Main Label(s)	Taka 貴
Export Label(s)	Taka
Homepage	https://www.domainetaka.com
Tours	available with reservations; limited English support

Nagayama Honke Shuzojo, housed in a beautiful and nationally registered "important cultural asset" Western-style building dating back to 1919, sits on the rural outskirts of industrial Ube City in western Yamaguchi. The small Koto River flows past the front door of its main office, while the drive to the brewery leads through rolling rice fields, many of which are now farmed by the brewery staff to grow rice for brewing.

Nagayama Honke has been making sake in this spot since 1888. The main label was originally Otokoyama—a name likely familiar to sake drinkers because there are over a dozen breweries using it, including Sanyo-Onoda's Nagayama Shuzo (yes, they're related)—until 2001, when current toji Takahiro took over. He saw that success outside of Yamaguchi would require a new label, and with advice from a sake retailer friend he settled on Taka, using the first

character from his own name. The kanji on the label was also his work, written with his non-dominant left hand.

Takahiro changed more than the label when he took over. "My first idea was to make junmai, but my father was against it," he says. "Sake brewers of his generation mostly looked down on junmai because they thought it resulted in overly acidic sake. Honestly, though, that was more about the limits of the brewers. They didn't know how to make proper junmai, but techniques have come a long way."

His persistence paid off, and he has made only junmai sake ever since. The label has won awards and popularity, but above all Taka is known for its balance and firm structure, in many ways influenced by Takahiro's enchantment with the wine world. He visited France with a wine-selling friend in 2007, and again in 2009, where he toured wineries following the *vin naturel* philosophy. He credits this with a major shift in his thinking about his own production and often references French winemaking when talking about sake.

"When I saw how deeply these small, but still successful, wineries valued nature, and drew a hard line on what can and can't be done in winemaking, it really impressed me. I realized we could do something similar when making sake."

One particular thing the toji picked up from the French vintners is the word "terroir," an idea that is right now sweeping the sake world—but not without controversy. This French word is often used in discussing wine, but few really agree on what it specifically means. Clearly, it's from the Latin root *terra*, so it evokes images of the land and the earth. In usage, it broadly encompasses the specific climate and topography that influence a wine's character, and thus is often used synonymously with "regionality" to designate similarities in style and flavor of wines from a given area. But in the sake world the term has yet to be accepted, simply because the connection between the natural world and the finished product is blurred.

Sake is very much a crafted product, not a natural one. The sake-making process is what gives sake its aroma, its flavor, and its style. The influence of rice and water is real, but so is the influence of temperature control, timing, yeast choice, and myriad other factors that are typically decided by the toji and not left up to the natural environment.

Even in those processes that Nagayama leaves to nature, there is a strong level of human control involved. For example, a significant portion of Taka consists of kimoto and yamahai shubo, which depend on bacterial fermentation action to produce lactic acid. Taka uses natural bacteria from the brewery—but it has been lab-isolated and packaged. Kimoto often requires long, hard work using wooden poles to crush rice into a paste, but Nagayama uses a mechanical drill equipped with a stirring attachment. In this way the natural elements are all helped along by human action. And all of these are decided by the toji, meaning Takahiro himself.

He readily admits this. He grins when I bring up the active role of a toji in sake making. "Of course, sake is a product of skill. I don't like to talk about it, as a toji myself, because it should be a given that the maker be skilled. So, it's the other parts that I focus on. For me, terroir is about everything around us that we don't usually think about. It's like water to a fish—we don't recognize it until we're outside it. It's the air, the water, the community, the light and temperature. We have to show gratitude for all of these things that allow us to make sake, when we are making it."

He adds that this is something he worries about with the current fad of hypermilling sake. "If you just keep polishing away the rice, then it isn't going into the sake. There's no gratitude there. It's almost spiritual. If you want a Japanese term for terroir, it might be *yao-yorozu no kami*, all the spirits of the land, water, and air. The rice has a spirit, and so does the water, and the soil."

One thing that stands out in all our conversations is that the terroir of the Taka label is not about the taste of sake, that is, about making a sake that is identifiable to the drinker from taste alone. It is far more abstract. "I'm trying to work out my own philosophy with this word. And there are differences, of course, from wine. In French *vin naturel* they put strict limits on all kinds of things like fertilizer and other artificial farming techniques, but I'm not so strict. The European conception of human action is that it somehow isn't part of nature, but in Japan we see that when you leave the wild landscape untouched, it can go out of balance. When humans work in the wilds, doing things like chopping wood and making charcoal with care and consciousness, that helps maintain balance." I comment that this idea seems rooted in the *satoyama* landscape of Japan—the patchwork of cultivated fields and tended wilds that also provide the necessities of life. He agrees. "I see human activity as part of nature, so there's no need to cut it out of the terroir of sake."

At the same time, Takahiro is very concerned about the

environment. "As I get older, my attitude toward sake making has changed. When I was in my thirties, I wanted to make the very best sake I could. Now, in my forties, I want to think more about reducing our food mileage and being more sustainable while we make it."

This is where Nagayama's other major winemaking influence comes in: the Domaine system. "I started Domaine Taka as a subsidiary to grow our rice locally." He takes me outside, and as we cross the Koto River flowing in front of the sakagura building he sweeps his arm across the fields around us. "These are ours. We still can't grow enough for all our needs, but we're getting closer." Nagayama grows Yamada Nishiki here, which he calls Ube Yamada Nishiki, and uses it in all sake sold under the Domaine label. He is also testing crops of Omachi rice and, if successful, will add Ube Omachi to his Domaine system.

The Domaine system, for Nagayama, is more than just a way to source rice and build some market identity. It is a way to help support local agriculture. "Helping build a market for Yamaguchi-grown Yamada Nishiki, and buying directly from farmers, puts more money in their pockets. Then, if those farmers get too old to work their fields, we can buy or lease them and handle the farming, so we are helping build for the future, too."

Nagayama Honke's dedication to rice goes even beyond its typical brewery needs. The company not only grows rice but has built a processing facility for drying, weighing, and grading, complete with the full complement of combines and tractors. It is rare indeed to see a sake brewery so serious about agriculture, and deeply gratifying for the respect it demonstrates to the local farmers who make that sake brewing possible.

The resulting sake is quintessentially local—not because of a particular Yamaguchi style or flavor but because the toji values those local connections and products. It is a product of a complex process, but the foundation is built on local soil, with local hands.

TOJI'S CHOICE SAKE

The Domaine Taka
Ube Yamaguchi

NAGAYAMAHONKE SHUZOJO CO.,LTD.
Since 1888
—— PRODUCT OF JAPAN ——

純米大吟醸 宇部山田錦

**Domaine Taka Junmai
Daiginjo 2019**
Seimaibuai: 50%
Rice: Ube Yamada Nishiki

Domaine Taka Junmai Daiginjo is the flagship sake for Nagayama Honke, with its Domaine label right on the front. It is a premium junmai daiginjo made from rice grown within five kilometers of the brewery by brewery staff. It is thus an encapsulation of toji Nagayama Takahiro's brewing ideals: sake as an expression of locality, rice grown and sake brewed in the same air, from the same water, in the same place.

The sake itself is rock-solid—aromatic and elegant. The Taka label is known for balance and for its expression of the minerality of its hard-ish water. Accordingly, this sake does not offer a silky-smooth mouthfeel, but rather a more assertive structure. It presents with a crisp dryness that is offset by mellow banana sweetness. It has a clean, balanced core of umami, and a medium finish that showcases that minerality. The overall character is best expressed as balance. All the elements work together in harmony.

Premium sake is often relegated to slow sipping and aromatic enjoyment, but to me this is a meal sake as well. Its solid structure and balanced minerality give it the backbone to stand up to all kinds of dishes. I would not hesitate to drink this with a steak, personally.

Northern Yamaguchi

Abu/Hagi 168

THE ABU/HAGI REGION on the northern coast of Yamaguchi is home to some of the oldest settlements in the prefecture. With Jomon village remains dating back some ten thousand years, followed by Yayoi period (300 BCE–300 CE) settlements, it is one of the places where paddy rice farming was first adopted on the island of Honshu. The Abu highlands are an area of fertile soils and heavy rainfall, and many of the hillsides are carved into terraced rice fields that produce high-quality rice for both eating and brewing.

Abu (population 3,085 as of 2022) is a small community that is essentially surrounded—and often overshadowed by—the more famous Hagi City. But Abu has plenty to offer in its own right. Its rural landscape is perfect for farming, and its produce is among the most highly prized in Yamaguchi.

Hagi (population 44,151 as of 2022) is a port in the north of Yamaguchi and probably the most famous city in the prefecture. It was here that modern Japan was born, as the politicians and zealots who led the Meiji Restoration gathered and studied in Hagi under Yoshida Shoin to learn the philosophy summed up in the slogan "Revere the emperor and expel the southern barbarians."

Hagi's historical importance goes back to the beginning of the Edo period, to 1600. The Mori clan sided with the Toyotomi clan against the Tokugawa armies. Although by staying out of the decisive battle at Sekigahara they ended up contributing to the Toyotomi loss, the victorious Tokugawa shogunate punished the Mori by confiscating most of their lands and thus cutting their vast income. Mori Terumoto, forced to move his capital away from Hiroshima, chose Hagi as the location for his new castle. Local legend says he picked Hagi because it sits on a delta, which reminded him of his former home in Hiroshima. Although he still ruled Nagato and Suo provinces, the finances of his clan never really recovered, and the seeds of resentment against the Tokugawa shogunate were planted.

Toward the end of the Edo period, Hagi became a hotbed for more than political reform. Its leading citizens studied in Europe and the United States and brought back ideas like the reverberating furnace to make better steel as well as military training that eventually helped the emperor's forces defeat the shogun's outdated armies. Many of the most instrumental people in that fight went on to become politicians and statesmen, helping to establish Yamaguchi as a source of more prime ministers than any other prefecture.

The long history of rice here, and the concentration of wealth the castle brought, means that this region has been a brewing center for centuries. One of Yamaguchi's toji guilds, the Otsu Toji, originated here and still influences brewing all over northern and western Yamaguchi. As of March 2021, the Japanese government has recognized this history and its modern iterations by awarding Abu and Hagi a Geographical Indication status, essentially a protected trademark. Now, any sake brewed with local water from rice grown in Hagi and Abu that passes a tasting process can be labeled with the GI Hagi indication.

Abu no Tsuru Shuzo
阿武の鶴酒造

Founded 1897

Kuramoto	Miyoshi Ryutaro
Toji	Miyoshi Ryutaro
Production	200 koku / 36 kiloliters
Main Label(s)	Abu no Tsuru 阿武の鶴, Miyoshi 三好
Export Label(s)	Miyoshi
Homepage	http://abunotsuru.jp/
Tours	not offered

Abu no Tsuru's brewery building is on a small, mostly shuttered commercial street in the small town of Abu, not far from the town's main train station. It is the only sake brewery still operating in the community, but for thirty-four years it was not even that.

Miyoshi Ryutaro, just thirty-seven years old at the time of this writing, is the fifth generation of his family to head Abu no Tsuru, but the business had shifted to liquor distribution by the time he was born. "No one was making sake here when I was a child. The sakagura was basically just a warehouse, then," he says.

How, then, did he ever think of restarting it? The answer is almost comically convoluted. "I went to Tokyo for university, and then I started working as an interior designer for clothing shops. After a while, though, I wanted to try something new. I checked the help-wanted ads and found one for a sake brewery in Chiba Prefecture," he says. Chiba is next to Tokyo, so he went for it. Surely, I ask, he had some ideas of continuing his own family business?

"Not at all. I never considered myself part of a brewing family. I wanted to try making things, though, and making sake sounded like interesting work." Miyoshi worked as a brewer for seven years or so, moving from Chiba to Saitama, then Gifu, Aomori . . . and finally, he says, a conversation with friends reminded him that his family did, technically, own a sake brewery. "I realized that the license was still there, and that made me think I should try to revive it."

Miyoshi returned home around 2015 (his memories are a little fuzzy around that period), but it took months of hard work to get the kura up and running. "It had been closed up and used for storage for thirty-four years. It took a whole year just to clean it out, then I had to get all the equipment together." More than anything, he was daunted by the economics. Brewing equipment is not cheap, but Miyoshi found support from many local kura. "Other brewers sold me used equipment at a huge discount, or out and out gave me some. And more than that, they advised me. President Sumikawa [of Sumikawa Shuzo/Toyo Bijin] even let me intern with him for a few months to become a better toji."

"Our local rice is high quality, and the farmers are our neighbors. Why wouldn't I use it?" After all, this part of Yamaguchi, the Abu highlands, is one of the first places where people started planting rice on the island of Honshu, meaning there is over a thousand years of rice-growing history right here. "All that rice is such a valuable resource that I want to treat every single batch with all the care I can."

This training was especially important because not only was Miyoshi planning to take over as kuramoto/toji, but he was going to do everything on his own. To this day, Abu no Tsuru is essentially a one-man operation, with part-timers helping out on really big jobs. Miyoshi makes all the koji, shubo, and mash on his own, and has done so ever since brewing started up again.

It was a slow start. After the year spent cleaning out the brewery, it took another year to gather finances, track down equipment, set it up, and practice. In the meantime, Miyoshi borrowed facilities at another brewery to begin producing his sake. He began full production at his own brewery in 2017, and with its first product Abu no Tsuru made an immediate splash in the sake world, not least of all because of the striking label designs.

"I want to make the very best sake I can. I see that as a way to repay all those who helped me get to where I am now. But I also care very much about design." Miyoshi called on help from a friend he had made during his time working in the interior design industry in Tokyo. "There are three of us. We work together on all the labels for the Miyoshi line, and there is meaning in everything," he explains.

He then goes through all the elements of the label, and it is like an ingenious puzzle box. (See the Toji's Choice section, below, for a look at the design.) First, the three bold horizontal lines. At first glance, for the Japanese speaker, this is obvious: It is the first character of the name. Miyoshi (the name of the sake and that of the brewer) consists of two Chinese characters, 三好, each with its own meaning. The first, 三, simply means "three." The second, 好, suggests meanings like benefit, something liked, love, and other positive things. Then, Ryutaro reveals a trick. Turning the bottle on its side turns the 三 character into three serif numeral 1s. "This represents each of the many trios that make up sake: rice, water, and koji. The *sandan jikomi* [three-stage fermentation]. The traditional belief that what makes good sake is first koji, second shubo, and third the ferment."

Then, the toji explains why they eventually settled on using his name. "Not only is the first character linked to all of the trios that are part of sake making, but there is an old Japanese saying that good business is *sanpo yoshi* 三方好, meaning that benefits flow in three directions: to the maker, to the seller, and to the buyer." Both characters of Miyoshi's name, and thus the label, are in that phrase, of course. Everything links ingeniously together. The label has won numerous awards in design competitions all over the world and is one of the most striking in the industry.

Of course, what is behind that label is what really counts to the sake lover, and Miyoshi makes his sake with deep care given to every element and part of the process. "All of the Yamada Nishiki I use is grown locally," he says, and points out that he was part of the committee that helped get Hagi and Abu GI certification. "Our local rice is high quality, and the farmers are our neighbors. Why wouldn't I use it?" After all, this part of Yamaguchi, the Abu highlands, is one of the first places where people started planting rice on the island of Honshu, meaning there is over a thousand years of rice-growing history right here. "All that rice is such a valuable resource that I want to treat every single batch with all the care I can." Miyoshi's fermentation is done at low temperatures, slow and long in the ginjo style, even if he does not always label the sake as such. "That's the way to get the sake flavors I aim for: clean, clear, with an identifiable rice character." This is, he says, an expression of the local Hagi style, and from the next brewing season his Miyoshi sake was eligible for the GI Hagi label.

> "Not only is the first character linked to all of the trios that are part of sake making, but there is an old Japanese saying that good business is *sanpo yoshi* 三方好, meaning that benefits flow in three directions: to the maker, to the seller, and to the buyer."

Another way that Miyoshi stands out from other Hagi-area brewers is in his active embrace of the foreign market. He is currently pursuing distribution to East Asian and North American consumers and is retooling the Miyoshi line to be his flagship international brand. To that end, he says, "I want to learn more about local food cultures so I can make sake that will match what people eat. I want my sake to be accessible, so that anyone who wants can pick up a bottle and enjoy it the way they want."

Finally, he points out a sort of simple verse written on either side of the label of Miyoshi Blue.

香レル想イ・海駆ケル
The scent of hopes, Sent across the sea.

This is an eloquent expression of the emotion he pours into his bottles, and what he hopes drinkers on distant shores will get when they open each one. Will they catch a scent of the passion and craft that goes into each sip?

One can only hope.

TOJI'S CHOICE SAKE

Miyoshi Green
Seimaibuai: koji 40% /
kakemai 60%
Rice: Yamada Nishiki

Toji Miyoshi Ryutaro says that Miyoshi Green was the first sake in the Miyoshi line to appear, and as such it encapsulates his original intention for the label. The combination of highly polished koji and less-polished *kakemai*, or mashing rice, is done as a kind of compromise. "The higher polish in the koji helps create more clarity and delicacy, but the lower polish of the mashing rice helps to bring depth, while also keeping costs down," he says. It is an attempt to bring a touch of daiginjo character to a lower-price-point sake, in other words.

"My intent is to evoke green fruits, like muscat and honeydew melon," Miyoshi says. This sake, then, brings an assertive acidity. "I wanted this to be a particularly good match for richly spiced cuisine like that of east Asia, or even of Italy. So, it has balanced acidity and umami, with less sweetness."

In my glass, I detected an initial lactic aroma, with the assertive acidity mentioned. It carried notes of yogurt, banana, and melon indeed. The initial sip also carried a lactic note but had a cleansing acidity and a firm backbone of umami that made it quite moreish. It is indeed a well-built meal sake and a testament to Miyoshi's brewing skills, and to his planning as well.

Iwasaki Shuzo
岩崎酒造

Founded 1901

Kuramoto	Iwasaki Kiichiro
Toji	Iwasaki Kiichiro
Production	300 koku / 54 kiloliters
Main Label(s)	Choyo Fukumusume 長陽福娘
Export Label(s)	Choyo Fukumusume
Homepage	https://iwasakishuzou.com/page/top-en
Tours	available with reservations; no English support on-site

Iwasaki Shuzo is on a shopping arcade right in the center of Hagi City, within walking distance of the castle town and museum district. This gives the brewery both a clear place in local daily life and an aura of history, of connection to Hagi's illustrious past. There are monuments to historical figures and pieces of old equipment used by the Hagi modernizers not a block from the brewery, but fifth-generation kuramoto/toji Iwasaki Kiichiro remains unmoved by the pressure all that history might exert.

"All I really care about is making delicious sake. The idea of being a 'Hagi Sake,' whatever that means, really doesn't concern me," Iwasaki says. What's important is what the location offers his brewing. The brewery is on what locals call the "triangle," the delta island formed where the Abu River splits into the Hashimoto and Matsumoto rivers. These feed an underground supply of soft water, which Iwasaki uses to brew Choyo Fukumusume. "The water is clean and soft, so it makes for relatively gentle, sweet

sake, but isn't too assertive on the flavor. That means I can focus on the rice."

And for Iwasaki, rice has become the ultimate key to delicious sake. Like many other Yamaguchi brewers, Iwasaki is taking a direct hand in the sourcing of his brewing rice. He is part of the Hagi Sakamai Migaki Kyodokumiai, or the Hagi Sake Rice Polishing Cooperative, an organization that grows and mills Yamada Nishiki for the six sake breweries in and around Hagi. The cooperative has begun to offer a full range of sake rice supply services: planting, harvesting, processing, milling, and distribution. Its hard work means that Hagi now has fields producing top-graded sake rice for local breweries to use in producing some of Yamaguchi's best sake. Iwasaki has been part of this initiative from the beginning.

He was also head of the committee that led the drive for Geographical Indication recognition for Hagi sake. GI is like a trademark for a local product—think Champagne vs. sparkling wine.

Hagi and neighboring Abu achieved that landmark status in March of 2021, and their success was due in no small part to the rice-growing efforts spearheaded within the cooperative. As a result, sake made from rice grown in the Hagi or Abu region, made (of course) with local water and matching a defined set of quality characteristics, can be officially labeled GI Hagi.

But why exactly is Iwasaki so intent on rice now?

"Rice is the heart of sake. The better you understand rice, the better you can brew," he says, with utter conviction. The extent to which Iwasaki now pursues this concept of brewing the ideal sake is almost single minded. He is the first in his line to take over both the kuramoto and toji jobs, and although he does not express any kind of grand ambition, his every effort is geared at bringing his kura and his process in line to reach his ideal sake profile. "We're renovating the *kojimuro* right now, and I'm working on increasing production, but just a little. I'd like to get over 500 koku, but I don't want to go past 1,000. It's hard to maintain quality at that level. What I'm really looking at is process." This drive for improvement is also driving a reassessment of the brewery's overall production style.

"We are small, and still have some futsushu and honjozo in production, but I'm just now trying to decide when to make the move to junmai-only," Iwasaki says. "Junmai brings more of the drinker's attention to the rice, and that's what I want to do." The sake he is aiming for is a pure expression of Hagi's rice, one that is above all "clean, clear, and rice forward." His efforts to bring the brewery's sake up to his personal standards mean that current production is already over 80% junmai.

Iwasaki has been in full charge of his family brewery since around 2017. Before that, he worked under previous toji, while the brewery still followed the traditional system. This had an unusual influence, since he trained under guild members of both Kumage Toji and the local Hagi region's Otsu Toji. His approach to brewing has thus been influenced by both Yamaguchi traditions, but he says that, more than anything, he is following his own intuition. "There are details that are different, like approaches to timing and koji style, but I don't really think about it much. I just try to make the best sake I can."

As I drink more of Iwasaki's main label Choyo Fukumusume, the picture of what that means is coming into sharp focus. Despite variations in rice, style, and expression, there is an identifiable commonality: The sake is clean, umami-centric, quick finishing, and easy to drink. The rice character is clearly at the core of this sake.

Because he is brewing in Hagi, which has a long tradition of sweet sake (much like its long tradition of sweet soy sauce), his sake tends to be sweet. But he is careful not to fall too far into the *nojun* category that is traditionally associated with this city. "*Nojun* sake can weigh you down sometimes, and more than anything I want sake that's easy on the palate." This is also where he thinks more about the people he is brewing for, rather than history or tradition. "I've inherited this brewery and its traditions, but more than that I've inherited the local customers,

"The idea of being a 'Hagi Sake,' whatever that means, really doesn't concern me," Iwasaki says. What's important is what the location offers his brewing. The brewery is on what locals call the "triangle," the delta island formed where the Abu River splits into the Hashimoto and Matsumoto rivers. These feed an underground supply of soft water, which Iwasaki uses to brew Choyo Fukumusume. "The water is clean and soft, so it makes for relatively gentle, sweet sake, but isn't too assertive on the flavor. That means I can focus on the rice."

the fans of Choyo Fukumusume. I have to serve them more than I have to serve the brewery."

When I ask him to outline just what he wants people to know about Iwasaki Shuzo and the sake he brews there, he says, "We don't make flashy, exciting sake. We make simple, delicious sake, and I hope people try it. I think they'll like it."

I certainly agree. Iwasaki describes his sake as "simple," but personally I find that overly modest. Not only is the label Choyo Fukumusume full of variation, but it offers a few shockingly good expressions. For example, the *hiyaoroshi* (pressed in spring, pasteurized once, then aged over the summer) balances perfectly the full-bodied depth expected from the style with an elegant sweetness usually seen in the ginjo class. The kimoto tokubetsu junmai, on the other hand, is one of the more understated but still powerfully structured kimoto I've tried. No matter which of the many variations of Choyo Fukumusume I drink, I am always presented with an eminently drinkable, interesting sake that pleases to the last drop.

Iwasaki Shuzo might not have the most dramatic story of Yamaguchi's sake breweries, but it perfectly reflects the dedication to craft and betterment that has driven the Yamaguchi "Jizake Revolution." Iwasaki is still evolving, and Choyo Fukumusume is sure to have a long, bright future because of it.

TOJI'S CHOICE SAKE

Choyo Fukumusume is currently establishing a strong reputation as a premium brewery, and this sake—Junmai Ginjo Muroka Nama Genshu Chokugumi—brings that new premium weight to bear. It also showcases the brewery's focus on natural rice character, which is fundamental to the GI Hagi identity. The Yamada Nishiki rice in this sake is all grown and milled in Hagi, and Iwasaki evokes that rice

**Choyo Fukumusume
Junmai Ginjo Muroka Nama
Genshu Chokugumi**
Seimaibuai: 40%
Rice: Yamada Nishiki

when brewing its sake, putting the full, creamy Yamada Nishiki character front and center.

As a daiginjo *chokugumi*, which means it was bottled directly from the press, this particular sake also gathers only the very best of the pressing. This reduces oxygen contact and keeps the sake in the very best condition. And offering the sake as muroka nama genshu means it reaches your glass in its cleanest, least-adjusted version.

As such, it is fresh, bright, and crisp. The nama flavors do not mask the sake's character, and balance is maintained to the last drop. It has a creamy, mochi-like sweetness and rice umami notes that give way to a clean, mildly astringent finish. It simply makes you want to keep drinking.

It is a dry sake for Yamaguchi, and the umami notes are mouth-wateringly delicious. It is the kind of meal sake that awakens the appetite as well, and neither overshadows nor loses out to even big flavors like Japanese curry or pork cutlet.

Nakamura Shuzo
中村酒造

Founded 1902

Kuramoto	Nakamura Masahiko
Toji	Nakamura Masakazu
Production	100 koku / 18 kiloliters
Main Label(s)	Takarabune 宝船
Export Label(s)	Takarabune
Homepage	http://shirouo.jp/
Tours	available with reservations; no English support on-site

Nakamura Shuzo stands just a few meters from the Ubakura Canal, a Hagi waterway built for flood control by the Mori clan during the Edo period. The canal is lined with fishing boats, and the smell of the nearby ocean fills the air. This is a distinctly seaside brewery, and fishing is in its blood. Toji Nakamura Masakazu clearly points out that connection, saying, "The full name of our label is Shirouo Takarabune. Hagi, and especially this canal, has always been known for the fish." "The fish" is a reference to *shirouo*, the ice goby, a tiny fish that grows no larger than a few centimeters and remains transparent its whole life. In Hagi these fish are scooped up by the thousands in spring and eaten—or rather drunk—swimming in soy sauce. "The boats that would come back with a load of *shirouo* were like treasure ships hauling fortunes back to port," he goes on. Takarabune means, of course, treasure ship.

"The sake we make was intended from the start for those local fishermen. We make dry, rich sake for drinking warm after a long

day at sea. About half our production is still futsushu sold locally," he says. I myself bought a paper-cup pack of that futsushu from an ancient sake vending machine in front of the brewery—the only futsushu-only vending machine I have ever seen. Clearly, Takarabune is a staunchly non-trendy sake. It has remained rich and dry throughout the premium boom of delicate, light sake, and even its ginjo-class sake is matured for depth and umami.

One noteworthy element of Nakamura's sake is use of the high-temperature starter method, *koon toka moto*. Rather than slowly creating a fermentation starter by allowing the koji in the starter to grow at its own pace and release sugar for the yeast to consume gradually, the starter mix is brought up to around 60 degrees Celsius for a sudden spike in sugar, then flash-cooled in an ice bath to allow the yeast to get to work. This brewery is the first I've seen in Yamaguchi that uses no other method, and I wondered why they chose it. Nakamura shrugs. "It's what we do. I learned it here and didn't really question why. But it is part of our sake brewing," is his answer.

Another mark of tradition in the brewery is the labeling. Takarabune has many labels featuring prominent figures from Hagi's history, old city maps, and names calling to mind the city's place as a historical and political center. "I don't know who made that decision, or why, but these have become part of our brand. We sell a lot of these to tourists at museums and such. But I don't know if we're any more focused on Hagi's history than any other brewery," Nakamura says. It becomes clear that "why" is not a question that has bothered the toji all that much. He is, however, very focused on "what."

What kind of sake does he want to make? "My aim, the sake I want, is sake that anyone can drink, with any meal, and think it's delicious. Sake is a meal drink, and if I can make something that does that job for everyone, I'm happy," he says. He also says that he has no plans to focus on junmai. "Aruten sake is more stable, and more suitable for drinking during meals. I personally like it more, so my goal is a really delicious honjozo with wide appeal."

Apart from that brewing goal, Nakamura also has distinct ideas about the future of his brewery and Hagi sake. "I think sake has the power to make people happy. That's what the name Takarabune actually means, right? Something that brings happiness. I want to live up to that name."

This is more than just lip service. The toji has concrete ideas. "The sake business is growing for us," he says. "Now, with GI Hagi, I think we sake breweries have a responsibility to bring those benefits to the whole community, not just keep everything for ourselves." The area was granted that designation in March 2021 and was the first in the Chugoku region of western Japan to be so recognized. "One way I'd really like to share is by training young people to become toji," he adds. "That's one of the ways sake breweries have always supported the local community, right? We can train a young person in a skilled trade so they can start a family and support them, and then all that goes right back into the community. I think we should start actively reaching out to the next generation to keep that cycle going."

This particular idea might have to do with his own history. "When I was young, I never thought I'd be making sake. I was the kuramoto's son, so I was going to run the business," Nakamura says. "My father said I should study business management, then, and I did. I also worked technical jobs for a subsidiary of [Japanese telecom giant] NTT and such." Nakamura's background, then, was not on the brewery floor. "But then the toji said he wanted to retire, and my father called me back to help out. When I came back, I started working with the toji and learning the job. I also took a three-month brewing course from the National Research Institute of Brewing early on. But it was never my plan to take over!" Circumstances, though, demanded, and he stepped up to the job.

His father still runs the company, although most management work also falls to Masakazu now. "I'm not technically kuramoto/toji at the moment, but I am responsible for much of the management as well as brewing. It's a lot of work," he says, and one gets the feeling he would like some help with it. That explains, perhaps, why he is so intent on training a replacement toji! Still, he has not taken any shortcuts like automating processes, making less-labor-intensive sake, or cutting corners on rice.

"We use processing-grade rice for our lowest-rank futsushu, so we can't be sure where it's from, but everything else is grown very locally. We use Isehikari grown in Nagato [next to Hagi], Saito no Shizuku grown in Mine to the east, and the Yamada Nishiki is all grown in Hagi." I express surprise at Isehikari. "Yes, it's pretty rare, right? I think there are only two or three breweries in Yamaguchi using it. It's really hard to brew with," he says with a grimace. He brews with it because the farmer who grows it made the request directly.

The local production means that Takarabune is also eligible

for the GI Hagi indication. "I have to be honest; I wasn't really sure what that all meant at first. But now that it's here, and we can use it, I think it's going to be good for the whole area." In the end, what he wants is for people to visit. "Come see us. Come try the sake. Come try the food." It will be good for Hagi, and it will be good for visitors.

Shirouo no Sato Takarabune Junmai Daiginjo
Seimaibuai: 35%
Rice: Yamada Nishiki

TOJI'S CHOICE SAKE

Nakamura Shuzo maintains its emphasis on traditional, dry sake from top to bottom. Shirouo no Sato Takarabune Junmai Daiginjo is a prime example. It is made with the legendary "YK35" specifications that dominated the premium-sake realm in the 1980s: Yamada Nishiki rice, Association yeast #9 (*kyokai kobo kyugo* in Japanese), and a seimaibuai of 35%.

On opening, it presents a big, airy aroma with notes of vanilla, mochi rice, and delicate floral hints. In the glass, it has a much more low-key stature. It is a dry, crisp sake, not at all the *nojun* style that Yamaguchi is known for. It has a touch of west-Japan sweetness, but it is overshadowed by an almost woody finish. The robust acidity makes it a reasonably good meal sake for meaty dishes, but it might struggle with spicier foods.

This is not a sake I expected from drinking other Takarabune expressions, which tend toward heavier, richer styles, and it displays a respectable versatility within the brewery. Brewing premium ginjo is still difficult for smaller breweries, but Nakamura has achieved with this particular one a distinct melding of premium-sake quality with its own take on traditional brewing.

Okazaki Shuzojo
岡崎酒造場
Founded 1921

Kuramoto	Okazaki Takahiro
Toji	Okazaki Yasushi
Production	600 koku / 108 kiloliters
Main Label(s)	Chomonkyo 長門峡
Export Label(s)	Chomonkyo
Homepage	https://www.chomonkyo.com/
Tours	not offered

Okazaki Shuzo is found just outside of Hagi City proper, surrounded by mountains, next to the spot where the Akiragi River joins with the Abu River. It is not, however, near the label design's inspiration, Chomonkyo gorge, which is much further upstream on the Abu. According to fourth-generation kuramoto Okazaki Takahiro, "The original brewery was there, but when they dammed the river we had to move. My grandfather opened this new brewery in 1970." That makes the structure one of the newer brewery buildings in Yamaguchi Prefecture,

Its design is quite unusual. The brewery is all housed in a single cinderblock building, its walls stained a deep charcoal color from use. The interior is essentially one large open space, with one small room for rice steaming, another for making shubo, and a koji room. Fermentation, pressing, storage, and bottling are all done in the same area. "It makes the process smoother. We arrange everything by time, so we can just work the tanks in order. It also makes for an interesting view."

清酒 長門峡
醸造元 ㈲ 岡崎酒造場

Okazaki leads me up to a platform at one end of the brewery, and indeed we can look out over the whole layout. The fermentation tanks are arranged in order by size, with a walkway between them for easy access. Larger storage tanks dominate the far end, and between the fermentation and storage tanks is the single small Yabuta-style accordion press. It all has the rational look of a factory floor, if on very small scale, and without any automation. I have not seen anything quite like it in the local sake world.

The brewery that produces Chomonkyo is tiny relative to the industry at large, but still larger than some local colleagues. The kuramoto has no plans to grow, though. "It's a fine line," says Okazaki, "I don't want to force any big increase in production because that could hurt quality, but we also have to make sure we can produce enough to keep everyone paid." His plan is to try to move production toward higher-priced premium sake, but he also finds it hard to refuse the steady demand for lower-earning futsushu. "I was thinking the pandemic would be a good chance to switch over to more ginjo- and daiginjo-class sake, but then our old futsushu customers came back for their regular orders. It's not like I can say no!"

That kind of steady local demand is what has kept so many small sake breweries afloat through decades of market turbulence. Now, though, with the premium classes of sake drawing so many new consumers, small size can seem almost like a burden. Small breweries like Okazaki have limited facilities, and the decision to increase one area of production means something else has to be cut—and that would mean alienating an existing customer segment.

The continued demand for Chomonkyo futsushu is no accident. The sake has built a solid local reputation for quality across all its expressions, particularly among a hard-core traditionalist base. "Our sake doesn't really follow modern trends. Even as a Hagi brewery, we tend toward drier sake. Our sake meter values tend to run +3 to +5. Even our premium sake do. Our driest sake is a *karakuchi* junmai at +7."

The guiding principle for Okazaki's emphasis on dry sake is matching local cuisine. "Hagi is a port town, with lots of fresh seafood. We want sake that doesn't overpower that food, that's not too aromatic or too sweet. So, we aim for clean, dry sake with a nice quick finish." Sweeter, more aromatic sake tends to be more assertive on the dinner table, and although Hagi has a reputation for sweet sake, Okazaki considers that a mere trend and keeps to his drier ways.

Many premium junmai daiginjo brews lean more toward elegant aromatics than flavor, but not Okazaki. Chomonkyo junmai daiginjo is a flavor-forward sake, and a dry one. It comes in at +4 SMV yet does not seem to suffer for its non-trendiness. It won Gold at the Annual Japan Sake Awards in 2021, a real feat for a small brewery like Okazaki. "We made that one for meals, as well. It's not just clean, or elegant, we made sure it had deep flavor, and solid umami," the kuramoto says. The brewery avoids modern yeasts like #1801 for just that reason. "We use only 9E or 9H," he says, which are Yamaguchi-unique variations on the traditional #9 yeast.

The Chomonkyo flavor, then, is a well-defined one, and something that the brewery focuses on no matter the rice—which is another aspect that Okazaki values. "Apart from a single tank made from Okayama-grown Omachi we make by request every year, all of the rice we use is grown in Yamaguchi. All of the Yamada Nishiki is grown in Hagi. It's even milled in Hagi," he says,

"Hagi is a port town, with lots of fresh seafood. We want sake that doesn't overpower that food, that's not too aromatic or too sweet. So, we aim for clean, dry sake with a nice quick finish."

and that means that all of the brewery's premium Yamada Nishiki sake is eligible for the new GI Hagi designation. "We want the flavor of rice to come through," he says, and the focus on local production creates a flavor that is pure Hagi. "Hagi sake might follow its own trends, but none of that matters. We stay true to our flavor, and it's all local. That's it."

It is this idea that Okazaki wants people to get from his sake. "There are lots of different styles out there, and even different expressions in those styles. Not everything has to be a light, sweet, fruity daiginjo," he says. There are expressions, like those in Chomonkyo, that bring rice flavor without adornment or ostentation and that serve to prop up any meal table. "We're starting to export more, and we even have one guy working on bringing our sake to Italy. He's picked one that will work with the food there," he says. Okazaki does not express any hesitation over the idea of matching his sake with flavors overseas. "Our sake is always made for the dinner table. It doesn't matter where that table is!"

He also wants his sake to be a session drink, where people can sit and socialize over a bottle without getting tired of refilling their cups. "More than anything, it shouldn't be obtrusive," he says. Chomonkyo is a supporting actor on the dinner table, not a headline act. Customers in China, Singapore, Malaysia, and Hong Kong are already enjoying this taste of Hagi, and Okazaki plans to show drinkers in Europe and North America his wares as well.

TOJI'S CHOICE SAKE

Chomonkyo

Chomonkyo Daiginjo
Seimaibuai: 40%
Rice: Yamada Nishiki

Chomonkyo Daiginjo brings the brewery's focus on stability over trendiness front and center. This is an example of the aruten daiginjo style, which has dominated the Annual Japan Sake Awards for decades. The use of added brewer's alcohol in premium sake is not about increased volume, as it may be in cheaper futsushu. Adding a bit of alcohol before pressing helps to bring out more of the alcohol-soluble aromatic elements and also lightens some of the heavier flavors that can appear in junmai sake.

This version did, indeed, win gold at the Yamaguchi Sake Awards and Japan Sake Awards in 2021 with that exact profile. It offers big, gorgeous daiginjo aromas with the usual Yamada Nishiki notes of vanilla, rice, honeysuckle, and mochi. In the glass, though, it is much more restrained.

It presents with light sweetness of honeydew melon, yellow peach, and reserved honey notes. The acidity is clean and fresh, and helps the finish fade quickly into a mild hint of ethanol that fades to nothing but a desire to refill. This is an elegant, balanced sake that moves at a level surprising for such a small brewery.

Sumikawa Shuzojo

23

澄川酒造

Founded 1921

Kuramoto	Sumikawa Takafumi
Toji	Sumikawa Takafumi
Production	2,500 koku / 450 kiloliters
Main Label(s)	Toyobijin
Export Label(s)	Toyobijin
Homepage	https://toyobijin.jp/
Tours	not offered; there is a direct-sales shop on-site

Toyobijin is, in a word, famous. Not as much as Yamaguchi's other big name, Dassai, but enough that any talk of Yamaguchi sake with drinkers in Japan is sure to bring it up. "Oh, yes, Yamaguchi sake! Dassai and Toyobijin are delicious!"

The story of how Sumikawa Shuzojo got to that point is as full of turns of fate as any Greek drama, if not quite as tragic.

The company was founded in 1921, making it quite young in the sake brewing world. It began as a local producer for local consumption, making standard futsushu under the label Midorimusume, and managed to continue doing so through the turbulence of World War II. Like most other Yamaguchi brewers, they rode the wave of success leading to the 1970s peak by supplying sake on spec to major brewers outside the prefecture and then fell back on their local base market to stay in business as sales dropped in the post-peak era. Their products remained an essentially local brew up until around the 1990s.

However, at one point sales dropped so low that the brewery faced an existential crisis. That was when former owner Sumikawa Takatoshi, father of current toji/kuramoto Sumikawa Takafumi, decided to make the pivot to more premium sake, along with shifting the focus to larger markets, i.e., Tokyo. The first junmai sake Sumikawa released was under the label Jipangu, and it was moderately successful, enough to keep the brewery alive a little longer.

It was around this time that Takafumi joined the company full time. As the owner's son he had always known he would eventually take over as kuramoto, but back then the idea of being a double kuramoto *and* toji was unheard of. His courses at university had covered brewing science, but Takafumi didn't get serious until after his graduation, when he took a training position with sake powerhouse Takagi Shuzo, maker of Juyondai. There he met the young kuramoto/toji Takagi Akitsuna, a pioneer in that dual role. Juyondai was just at the beginning of its rise, and Sumikawa saw firsthand how combining the roles of owner and brewer could result in more control over how, and particularly what, the company put on the market. "That was the first time I ever thought I wanted to actually make my own sake," he says.

After his internship at Takagi, Takafumi returned to Yamaguchi in 2001 to work at the family brewery. He was a kurabito, or regular staff, there until the aging toji was ready to retire, at which point he took up the mantle. Soon after, he revitalized the company's sake under the Toyobijin label and pivoted entirely to premium *tokuteimeishoshu* sake.

Things went well. Sales in large urban markets began to grow, and Toyobijin began to earn a name for quality throughout Japan.

And then disaster struck.

Sumikawa is located in the mountains, between a steep hill and a small river. It is a lovely area full of clean water and green trees, but it is a bad place to be in a flood. In July 2013, a torrential rainstorm hit Yamaguchi and Shimane prefectures. The area around Mt. Tokusagamine, which includes Sumikawa Shuzo, recorded 450 millimeters of rain, over 17 inches, in just a few hours. The damage was massive: 189 buildings were destroyed, and nearly 2,000 flooded.

Sumikawa lost almost everything. The kura buildings remained, but equipment, rice, sake stock, and tanks of moromi were all lost. Sumikawa was faced with a terrible decision. Just enough was left to justify trying to rebuild and continue making sake, but enough had been lost to justify giving up. Sumikawa himself says, "We were at zero. It would have been easy to give up, since rebuilding would mean going from zero back into the hole, but I couldn't do it."

The flooding was huge news, and as a popular sake brewery Sumikawa was a focus of media attention. "I accepted every offer that came. It was exhausting, dealing with the press while rebuilding, but I felt like I owed it to the community. So many people had lost everything, even more than we had. I felt like we could bring attention to the devastation and maybe help that way," Sumikawa says. It worked, apparently, because help began pouring in both for the brewery and the local community.

"We never would have recovered on our own. It was the community at large that saved us," he says. As word spread of the damage, fans of the brewery began to gather from all over the country. In the end, more than a thousand people offered their time, money, and labor to help make sure Sumikawa was able to return to brewing. One of those was Fukumoto Takuo, a local rice farmer who had just begun growing Yamada Nishiki. He made the decision to shift a shipment of rice he had promised to another brewery to Sumikawa to supply the first batch after the flood, and that decision created a bond that lasts to this day. It is commemorated each year with a special batch brewed with Fukumoto's rice and labeled under the name Kanki 環起, meaning "Return."

And Sumikawa did return. As the brewery came back to full production, sales grew even faster than before, and in an interesting turn, Toyobijin's market shifted. "After the flood, Yamaguchi Prefecture became our main market. For some reason, maybe because of the media attention, maybe because of some kind of loyalty people felt after helping us rebuild, now 70% of our sales are inside the prefecture."

One event that must have helped came in 2016. That summer, Japan's Prime Minister Shinzo Abe hosted Russian President Vladimir Putin for a summit meeting at Otani Sanso, an elegant hot-spring hotel in central Yamaguchi Prefecture. The sake served at dinner was Toyobijin.

"I had no idea it was going to happen. Otani Sanso always order from us, and they did increase the order the month before, but I didn't think anything of it. Then, the day after, I got a call from [Japanese television broadcaster] Fuji TV asking about the foreign office's announcement. That was the first I heard about it!" Just as

President Obama drinking Dassai with former Prime Minister Abe was key in that sake's huge later success, this international sake sharing thrust Toyobijin into an enormous spotlight.

The period since has seen Toyobijin become strongly ensconced in the sake world. It is a favorite both within Yamaguchi and without, as people flock to its eminent drinkability and the elegance found in every variation.

Toyobijin is not a purely junmai brand, unlike other premium labels. Sumikawa explains: "When you allow yourself to add alcohol, you increase your options of flavor control. Consider that you can add up to 400 liters of alcohol to a single tank of moromi. Taken in single-liter increments, this gives you the power to create 400 different variations of that one single fermentation. How can I resist that?"

This is one more block of the basic tenet of Toyobijin sake making: Make sake people like to drink. As a philosophy this sounds simplistic, but compared to how other makers wax poetic over water hardness or rice strains, it can be almost refreshing. At heart, Sumikawa is all about his customers.

"All I want, at the end of the day, is to make sake people like," he says. To this end he has released special bottlings—particularly with the introduction of Jundo Ichizu, the latest incarnation of Toyobijin. The new sub-label, a follow up to Ippo, was introduced in spring of 2020, during the Covid-19 pandemic. The fermentation was already in process when everyone was ordered to stay home and avoid going out to bars or restaurants, and Sumikawa could read the writing on the wall.

"I wanted to help the only way I could think, with sake." He rushed bottling and shipping and sent out a Jundo Ichizu Junmai Ginjo for May—priced at an astonishing ¥900 a bottle (roughly US$8.00). "I put it out in hopes of people drinking it at home and finding some kind of pleasure in the middle of everything."

As a gesture, it hit home. People ventured out of their homes to buy it, so the sake shops that had struggled to fill the hole left by government pandemic restrictions were able to keep some sales moving. In the larger scheme of things, the sake may not have had a huge impact, but as a resident of Yamaguchi I can say it has left an impression on me, at least.

The label name is also significant. Sumikawa explains that every sub-name he uses has some significance, such as Kanki mentioned above. "I view the name as a reflection of our progress. The beginning of the journey was Jipangu—Japan itself. Toyobijin was reborn with Kanki, the return, and with Ippo [one step] we moved further down the path. Now, with Jundo Ichizu, we reflect on the single path, the path of brewing, we have followed. It actually came from the last bit of advice the former toji gave me before I took over. I asked him what I should focus on, and he said, simply *jundo ichizu,* which means follow the path of brewing."

When I ask Sumikawa about what he sees coming next on that path, he has a surprising answer. "I don't think about it. I don't make plans. We've faced collapse twice, and I know that plans can never survive reality. So, silly as it sounds, I just take every day as it comes."

It doesn't sound silly at all, I think. And the results speak for themselves.

TOJI'S CHOICE SAKE

Toyobijin, no matter the variation, has a reputation for supreme drinkability. The latest label, Jundo Ichizu, is one of the smoothest, most drinkable sake I've ever had, while Kanki offers a drier, more full-bodied flavor for those looking for something on another end of the scale.

For this introduction, kuramoto/toji Sumikawa Takafumi selected

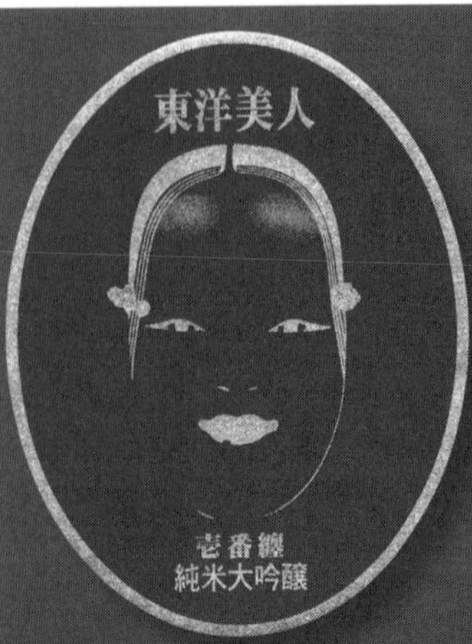

東洋美人

壱番纏
純米大吟醸

**Toyobijin Ichiban Matoi
Junmai Daiginjo**
Seimaibuai: 40%
Rice: Yamada Nishiki

his flagship bottle, Ichiban Matoi Junmai Daiginjo. The name Ichiban Matoi literally means "first battle standard," or, in other words, the flagship. This sake is the culmination of Sumikawa's brewing skill. It is made from Yamada Nishiki milled to 40% and is processed without charcoal filtration and only a single pasteurization to balance stability with untouched sake quality.

The sake presents a bright, vibrant ginjo aroma, with notes of fresh apple and pear. It hits the palate with a delicate mouthfeel, but it is not fragile. The elegant sweetness is balanced by a firm backbone of umami. The finish is clean, and mildly acidic, with a light hint of astringency. It is complex, interesting, and of course eminently drinkable.

For Sumikawa, this sake leans toward the dry, as the sweetness is quite subdued, and the finish is light and clean. Despite the lightness and daiginjo elegance, it has the backbone to stand up to a hearty meal. It is, in other words, an ideal showcase of all the skill that makes Toyobijin such a local favorite.

Yachiyo Shuzo
八千代酒造

Founded 1887 (as Kaba Shuzo)

Kuramoto	Kaba Kumiko
Toji	Kaba Kumiko
Production	150 koku / 27 kiloliters
Main Label(s)	Yachiyo 八千代, La+ Yachiyo Room
Export Label(s)	none
Homepage	https://ec.yachiyo-sake.com
Tours	available with reservations; no English support on-site

Yachiyo Shuzo stands on a narrow side road in rural Hagi surrounded by a few houses, some shuttered shops, and rice fields. This small brewery is now being run by fifth-generation head and brewer Kaba Kumiko. Kaba returned to the family brewery in 2017 but only recently took over as sole manager and brewer for the 2020 brewing year. She is also in a doubly rare position: not only is she a kuramoto/toji, still relatively unusual in Japan, she is also one of the relatively few women in complete charge of a sake brewery. The challenges she faces must be enormous.

Kaba recognizes the significance of all of this and takes her position seriously. In addition to preserving and helping to evolve her family sake brewery, she is active in the Kura Josei Summit, an organization that unites women in the sake industry to discuss the issues they face and to learn from each other. She also organizes a group called Marble, which is made up of local women working with fermentation and food cycles to encourage sustainability and

reduce waste. Much of Marble's work involves using waste from the sake industry, including the lees and rice bran from milling, in new foods. Kaba is not only supporting other women in the industry but helping to connect those outside it as well.

Kaba came into her role relatively unexpectedly. "I'm the oldest of three sisters," she explains. "We had decided that my younger sister, the middle child, would be taking over the brewery when the time came. So, I went to Tokyo to study and work." She became a nutritionist, while the middle sister went to Tokyo University of Agriculture, where a great many kuramoto and toji go to learn the brewing trade. However, the kuramoto in training did something that perhaps should have been a foreseeable possibility for a young woman venturing into the wider world: She fell in love, got married, and had a child. She gave up her brewing dreams and moved with her husband to be close to his family.

And so, the elder Kaba sister was faced with the choice of either learning to do things on her own or letting the family business fail. "I actually talked it over with my drinking friends in Tokyo. They all agreed it would be too sad to see another brewery close, especially since the difficulty of getting a new brewing license means there are so few new ones." She chose the hard path. She quit her job, moved back to Yamaguchi, and went through an intense six-month apprenticeship at Toyobijin brewer Sumikawa Shuzo as a crash course in becoming a toji, studying directly under kuramoto/toji Sumikawa Hirofumi. "There are a lot of young people who learn brewing there. President Sumikawa is very supportive of the younger generation, and I have been able to continue training and working there to practice and learn things like making koji."

As part of her training, she came up with her own brew recipe and released it under the new label La+ Yachiyo Room. It was an immediate hit and is now part of Yachiyo's permanent lineup, although it is still brewed at Sumikawa's facility. "I was happy to be able to create a sake that is entirely my own," she says. "After I came back from Tokyo, I was thinking about all the women I knew there, working hard all day and then going home to relax with a drink. I wanted to make something for them, something aromatic, relaxing, and easy to drink. Something to make evenings enjoyable." From the sales and reviews, it seems she hit the mark. It brings modern, stylish labeling to the traditionalist brewery's lineup at the same time it focuses on a more modern and light aromatic brewing style for easy drinkability. The new sake has maintained its popularity and regularly sells out soon after delivery. All of this is testimony to the power of innovation and to the value of a new perspective on sake brewing.

One thing the new brew does share with Yachiyo's older lineup is a focus on local rice. All of Yachiyo's rice is grown within Hagi's city limits, and 10% of that in the brewery's own fields by brewery staff. The trend toward sake breweries growing their own rice is still fresh, but it is one that Yachiyo embraced years ago. That, combined with the connection with local contract farmers, keeps the brewing solidly rooted in the community.

As a local brewer with a long history of local consumption, Yachiyo continue to produce a lot of sake outside the modern ginjo fruity trends. Their BD-14, for example, brings *yondan jikomi* production—"four-stage mash building," in which an extra step of koji and water are added to boost sweetness, more typical of futsushu—to a junmai style, resulting in a deep, complex, and richly sweet sake that evokes traditional Hagi flavor without the excessive additions of sugars or flavorings that many people find offputting. "The BD-14 is a label my father came up with. He wanted to find a balance between new junmai sake and the old-fashioned flavors. I did change things a little when I took over, and I think I cleaned up the flavors a bit," Kaba says with a grin. The brewery also produces a futsushu for local drinkers, as well as a junmai brewed with Yamaguchi cherry-blossom yeast and a few super-premium bottles.

In Kaba's mind, this is just the beginning. "There is so much I want to do. Now that I'm off to a solid start, next up is to improve equipment." The brewery is fairly old, and much of its equipment is distinctly obsolete. "We don't even have any cooling mats," she says, speaking of the tube-lined plastic mats that are wrapped around fermentation tanks and use running cold water to help control temperatures for ginjo fermentation. "We have one thermal tank for a few batches of ginjo a year, but that's just not enough." More equipment is what she needs to increase production, so that she can put her sake into more glasses.

Kaba herself was a sake lover long before she was a brewer, and so her end goal is to share that love. "I just want drinkers to know how versatile sake can be, and how delicious," she says. "There are so many variables, and so much to explore, I hope drinkers all over the world can get a chance to try for themselves."

TOJI'S CHOICE SAKE

La+ Yachiyo Room
Seimaibuai: koji 40% /
kakemai 50%
Rice: Yamada Nishiki

La+ Yachiyo Room is kuramoto/ toji Kaba Kumiko's first independent recipe, and she shot for the moon right from the start. A complex junmai ginjo with mixed seimaibuai, it requires the kind of equipment that her own brewery simply doesn't have. She still borrows cooled tanks and a modern climate-controlled koji room at Sumikawa Shuzo to make it.

"When I get the facilities, I'll make it here, but until then I need the temperature control at Sumikawa," says Kaba. The goal, she says, is an aromatic, fruity, smooth ginjo.

That profile is thoroughly within the modern style of aromacentric, light drinking sake. For Kaba, who came at sake brewing almost out of the blue, this is how she approaches people who might not normally consider sake as a drink: young, urban professional women. That is also reflected in the unusual label design—note the almost total lack of Japanese characters—and naming. "The name is meant to evoke a room of one's own, like a place of refuge from the stress of life."

La+ Yachiyo Room opens up with clean fruity aromas, as you would expect from a modern junmai daiginjo. The bright aromas give a good indication of what will come in the glass. The sake starts with juicy fruit salad notes of green apple, mango, and lychee. They are balanced out by the smooth rice-y umami that Hagi sake aims for, while the medium finish trails off with a mouth-cleaning hit of acidity that leaves you wanting more.

This is the kind of sake that works best with good conversation with friends, rather than over a meal or alone on your deck. It's a relaxing sake that adds a note of fun to evening drinking, and is the kind of drink that evokes comment, rather than contemplation. It's a bottle of fun!

connections

Ceramic Artists

Sake has been a part of Japan's food culture for centuries. Even when the common population did not have ready access to it, the upper classes regularly enjoyed drinking at meals and garden parties, as can be seen in any number of paintings and prints from Japan's feudal period. Those same pictures reveal something else fundamental to the nation's food culture: pottery.

Japan has one of the world's most vibrant ceramic art cultures, and the way it blends seamlessly into everyday life is hard to believe for someone coming from a place like the United States, where making pottery is more of a hobby and occasional artform than a source of daily goods. Here in Japan, I can walk into a small-town general store and find a selection of ceramicware, made in Japan by hand in mass quantities, for a few dollars per piece. Even discount "¥100 shop" chains have Japan-made pottery for sale. I can also go to a local pottery studio's gallery and buy fine ceramicware—meant for real use in real kitchens—for several hundred (or thousand!) dollars.

This ubiquity includes sake vessels, called *shuki* in Japanese. Appreciation of Japanese pottery as an artform usually focuses on tea ware for the traditional *sado* tea ceremonies, but for many ceramics lovers in Japan, shuki is the gateway drug, as it were. The variety is immense—*tokkuri* flasks, tiny *ochoko* or large *guinomi* cups for drinking, saucer-like *sakazukui* used at formal occasions, and beaker-like *katakuchi* pitchers. There are so many unique forms and colors that there are even mass-market books dedicated to exploring individual shapes and styles.

Pottery in Japan is a highly regional art. There are cities and

Hagiyaki sake vessels

prefectures all over the country that have centuries-old reputations for pottery making. And Yamaguchi Prefecture just happens to be one of the most famous of these, with the Hagiyaki wares of Hagi City.

There is an old saying in the tea-ceremony world, "First Raku, second Hagi, third Karatsu," ranking these famous pottery traditions known for their prized tea ware. Raku is a very old style centered around a single family in Kyoto, while Karatsu is a Korea-influenced style found in Kyushu. And Hagi is here, in Yamaguchi.

Hagiyaki (the suffix -*yaki* literally means "cooked" and refers to fired ceramic ware) found its start, as so many western Japanese pottery styles did, with Korean potters brought here after Japan's military invasions in the late 1500s. In 1604, the local lord Mori Terumoto brought two potters—brothers Yi Sukkwang and Yi Kyeong—from Korea to Hagi, where they established kilns to make pottery for the nobility.

Since then, the Hagi style has evolved into a unique expression, even in Japan. Traditional Hagiyaki, called *himehagi* or "Princess Hagi," often has warm, almost soft tones brought out from the natural shading of the relatively coarse local clay, and glazes with gentle colors like pale salmon, white, and light blue. One of the defining characteristics of the style is a phenomenon called *hagi no nanabake*, or the "seven transformations of Hagi." The glaze is webbed with tiny cracks, or crazing, which allow tea or sake to slowly seep into the porous clay. This causes the pottery to shift in color over the years as substances in the tea react with the clay's mineral content. These subtle changes, and the natural tones of the clay and glaze, are the basis of its popularity in the tea world.

Hagiyakai has not remained a purely traditional tea style, though. Kaneta Masanao, eighth-generation potter at Tenchozangama kiln in Hagi, says that "after World War II, the children of the potter families started going to university and studying art. When they came back, then, they had new ideas about creativity and freedom that were restrained by traditional craft. Here in Hagi, the Miwa potters in particular were the vanguard of a new way of thinking." He explains that Miwa Jusetsu (who uses the adopted title Kyusetsu XI for his art) saw the work being done by artists in Kyoto and other increasingly creative pottery centers and was inspired to explore new expressions in his pottery. This is how Kyusetsu XI created *oni hagi* ("devil Hagi")—a style that eschews the traditional softness of Hagiyaki with thick, clumped white glaze over heavy black clay.

Hagiyaki is thus both a traditional craft known for practical vessels and a space for creative exploration of ceramics as an art form. In both cases, as art and craft, shuki are a common creation.

Hadano Hideo, forty-nine, is the son of Yamaguchi Prefecture Living Cultural Treasure Hadano Zenzo and a potter at Hadano Shigetsu Gama kiln. His work naturally includes tea ware, as well as flower vases, jugs, and decorative pieces, but the man himself loves to make shuki, because he is a sake lover. "Whenever I'm making a *guinomi* I imagine how sake will taste from it, and how the shape of the rim will feel on the lips. Then, after firing, I always test one out myself!" He gets a bottle of his favorite sake to give freshly fired *guinomi* a full test and fills *tokkuri* sake flasks to see how smoothly they pour. "I don't see a piece as finished without use. A plate isn't a plate until you put food on it. How does the food sit? How does it look against the pottery? That's all part of what I consider when I'm making something." Hadano thus represents the practical side of the art of pottery, making items for use that bring a touch of aesthetic sense and pleasure into daily life.

The more artistic creators

of Hagiyaki also work in shuki. Kaneta's work at Tenchozan-gama is far more abstract and challenging than most of that coming out of Hadano Shigetsu kiln. He uses an unusual technique called *kurinuki*, in which he beats a piece of clay into shape with wooden paddles then digs out the interior to create a vessel, rather than doing turning on a wheel. The result is a style with a distinct sense of mass—thick, heavy pieces made of intersecting planes and irregular shapes. And yes, he makes shuki.

"I personally prefer to drink from porcelain," Kaneta says, "because this stoneware can be too porous. It soaks up the sake." I ask him if this isn't the very essence of Hagi's *nanabake*. "Yes, yes, sure, but the real *nanabake* takes a hundred years." In all things, Kaneta puts the aesthetic first. "I expect the user to put up with the pieces I make. I have to admit, some of my cups can be difficult to drink from. Like this *guinomi* in particular. I can imagine after a couple of drinks you might just get mad at it and throw it at the wall!" he says, showing me a cup with a triangular profile and a heavy, uneven rim. It does, indeed, look like it might be a challenge to use, but the visual element is so striking that it makes up for the vessel's impracticality. Which is, of course, exactly what Kaneta intends.

Whether you prefer tradition or art, Hagi's potters offer sake flasks and cups of enormous variety and high quality. There are kilns and pottery shops located all over the city, and any walk or drive will surely turn up a place with shelves worth perusing.

The search for shuki is not limited to Hagi. There are small pottery shops scattered all over Yamaguchi, so wherever you go, you should keep an eye out for the word うつわ or 器 (*utsuwa*) on a shop, which indicates there is pottery inside. And where there is pottery, there are shuki to explore.

A prime example can be found in Hikari City's Murozumi district, once a bustling shipping port. Now, it is a quiet seaside area with coffee shops, museums, and the Jaeho Choi gallery. Choi is a Korean-born potter who crafts his unique style of white porcelain in the mountains of Shunan. Choi is making waves in the art world with his larger works, like huge white-and-black moon jars and austere wall-mounted flower vases, but he also has treats for the sake drinker. His shuki include wildly original *guinomi* cups and *katakuchi* pitchers that contain a tiny, hand-painted figurine of a man in a kimono-like robe standing right in the middle. Each piece displays a different pose, but all the figures have a big, goofy grin on their faces. Choi says, "I was drinking one day and thought it would be fun to have a little doll in my cup so I would never have to drink alone." The effect is delightful, bringing a smile with every sip. "When you fill the vessel, it's fun to think about how much to pour. Is he going to have a sake

Kaneta Masanao

bath today? Or just wade in it up to his knees? Or maybe you pour up to his mouth, so he gets a sip, too?" Despite the serious intent of his art, it's clear Choi's work has more than a touch of whimsy, too.

Exploring ceramic drinking and serving vessels is a fun, and satisfying, way to expand your love of sake. Just, be careful. It can be a bit addictive!

Caring for fine ceramic shuki

Many of the more refined (and expensive) styles of Japanese pottery can be porous and absorb sake. While this will not directly damage the cup or flask, excessive absorption can lead to off aromas and even mold. To help prevent this, fill the vessel with warm water and let it soak for around ten minutes before use. Soon after you're done, wash the pottery and allow it to dry thoroughly in the open air before storage.

Travel
Information

Visiting Yamaguchi

Getting to Yamaguchi

Yamaguchi has reasonably good access by shinkansen. Tokuyama Station is a stop for the fastest Nozomi and Sakura shinkansen trains; stations served by the slower express trains are Shin-Iwakuni, Shin-Yamaguchi, Aso, and Shin-Shimonoseki.

Iwakuni Kintaikyo Airport, Yamaguchi Ube Airport, and Hagi-Iwami Airport (technically in Shimane Prefecture) have daily flights from Haneda Airport in Tokyo. All of the airports have bus connections to train stations on the local JR lines.

For more detailed guidance, check the official tourist websites:
https://www.visit-jy.com/en/plans

Getting Around Yamaguchi

Public Transportation

While Yamaguchi is far less served by public transport than more urbanized prefectures, an extensive if infrequently run network of buses fills the gaps left by the lack of train lines connecting the coasts. There is also a convenient Yamaguchi Bus Pass to help make travel easier.

For information, check:
https://www.oidemase.or.jp/secondary-traffic/en/
For bus pass information and possible routes, check:
http://www.visit-jy.com/model_route_guide/en/
Bus maps are here:
http://www.solasi.com/ymgbus/files/language/EN_busmap_202201.pdf

DRIVING

Driving in Yamaguchi is highly recommended. It offers much more access to the scattered attractions and sake breweries. Perhaps most attractive are the opportunities at sidetracks, like the many fantastic *michi-no-eki* 道の駅 (roadside stations) alongside surface roads that sell local produce, handicrafts, and the ubiquitous local sake.

You can get an English driving guide by PDF here:

https://www.oidemase.or.jp/secondary-traffic/en/download/panf.pdf

Places of Interest for the Traveler and Sake Lover

The cities and towns of Yamaguchi have more than just sake breweries. There are museums, cultural spots, historical landmarks, castles, and more just waiting to enchant. Here are some recommendations from someone who has lived in, and traveled around, Yamaguchi for much of his adult life.

IWAKUNI

The five wooden arches of Iwakuni's most famous landmark, **Kintaikyo bridge,** inspired both the name and label design of one of Yamaguchi's biggest local breweries, Gokyo ("five bridges"); the clean, soft water from the Nishiki River's underground flow is also used by the three breweries clustered in town. It is no exaggeration to say this is the true heart of Iwakuni, and one of the most well-known bridges in Japan, well worth any visitor's time to see. The surrounding area makes superb use of early spring's cherry blossoms and late fall's foliage to create a natural background for the bridge, and when the scenery is at its peak the parkland along the river is filled with festival-style food stalls, stages, and lanterns illuminating the trees.

Those who drive to this spot can park in a gravel lot by the riverside (¥300), while plane and train travelers can take one of the frequent buses from Kintaikyo Airport, Iwakuni Station, or the Shin-Iwakuni shinkansen station. Walking across the bridge requires a ticket. Basic round-trip tickets are ¥310, while a combination ticket including a ride on the ropeway up to the castle as well as entrance to the castle museum is ¥970. The bridge is always open. Payment after the ticket office closes in the evening should be left in the ticket office drop box.

After you cross the bridge toward the castle you'll find a cluster of shops selling snacks and souvenirs to serve tourists going on to visit **Kikko Park**. The park itself is worth a full day of exploration. Apart from its open plazas, beautiful trees, and statues, it has several museums, both public and private, that showcase local history and arts. Some of the best are:

Iwakuni Art Museum (9:00 to 17:00, no fixed closed days, ¥800 admission) has a collection of samurai armor and weapons, local glassware and ceramics, and other historical artifacts housed in a tall, white building reminiscent of traditional castle architecture.

Kikkawa Museum (9:00 to 17:00—last entry 16:30, closed Wednesdays except on national holidays, then the following day, ¥500 admission) is in a sprawling samurai manor and holds many possessions once owned by the ruling Kikkawa clan itself. There are weapons, armor, documents, and furniture.

Gokyo Bunko (10:00 to 16:00—last entry 15:30, closed Wednesdays and Thursdays, ¥700 admission, ¥1,000 for some special exhibits) is a small private museum run by Sakai Shuzo, the brewers of Gokyo sake. It has no permanent collection but displays temporary exhibitions connected to the history and culture of Iwakuni. The highlights for me are the shuki sake vessels around the entrance—all of which are made by local artisans and some of which are for sale. Find it by going right as soon as you cross Kintaikyo bridge and follow the river to a very steep down-sloping road. Take it down, and

Iwakuni's Kintaikyo bridge with cherry trees in full bloom

the museum, which resembles a two-story white house, will be on the corner.

Iwakuni Castle at the top of Mt. Shiroyama is also open to the public as a museum (9:00 to 16:45—last entry 16:30, ¥270 admission) with displays of more armor, weapons, and scrolls from the Kikkawa clan's treasure house. The highlight for me is the view from the top. Be warned, though, the interior is authentically built (although it is a 1960s reconstruction) and spaces can be very cramped—and the stairs very steep. You can reach the top of the mountain by a rather winding hike, or you can take the ropeway from Kikko Park (¥560 round trip). Check the ropeway hours carefully, as they vary a lot due to maintenance.

Drinking Iwakuni

If you would like to do a taste test of all five of Iwakuni's sake breweries at once, the best place is **Honke Matsugane** (1-7-3 Iwakuni, Iwakuni 741-0062), a general tourist facility on the town-side of the river near Kintaikyo bridge.

Honke Matsugane is in an old medicine-merchant house a short walk down residential streets from Kintaikyo bridge (it can be hard to find so I recommend asking your smartphone for directions). They offer samples of two sake from each of the five breweries using their own unusual ticket-vending-machine system. They also have a selection of small accompaniments (commonly called *sakana* 肴 in Japan, which is confusing because it sounds like the word for fish) made with local ingredients. My personal recommendation is *karashi renkon*, a dish made with local-specialty lotus root coated with spicy *karashi* mustard. They have displays of sake and materials from all five breweries, as well as videos introducing the sake-making process. And for a full castle-town tourist experience, you can make reservations to try on (replica) samurai armor for a photo session against the bridge. English support is available.

Another excellent drinking spot is **Mitsukanya** (1-3-15 Marifu, Iwakuni 740-0018, open 9:00 to 20:00 Monday–Saturday, 9:00 to 19:00 Sunday), a souvenir and liquor shop across from Iwakuni Station. They stock an excellent selection of Iwakuni and Yamaguchi sake and in the evening host a standing bar where customers can taste the wares by the glass.

SHUNAN/KUDAMATSU

Shunan City Museum of Art and History (10-16 Hanabatakecho, Shunan 745-0006, 9:30 to 17:00, last entry 16:30, closed Mondays, ¥200 admission) features more art than history, but it does have a permanent exhibit of pictures, panels, and artifacts related to local history to help contextualize the area's importance. The more interesting part of this museum is the exhibit of local artists and photographers like Sawano Bunshin, Hayashi Tadahiko, and others. It is accessible by bus from Tokuyama Station.

Unfortunately, most of the historical architecture in Shunan has been lost. As a former domain capital under the Mori clan it once had a castle, but all that remains are some of the worked stones from its construction scattered around the zoo and cultural hall near the Shunan City museum. The nearby shrine, **Yusui Jinja** (5854-7 Tokuyama, Shunan, Yamaguchi 745-0851), which dates back to 1811, venerates the spirit of clan lord Mori Naritaka.

Toishi Hachimangu shrine (2-3-1 Toishi, Shunan 745-0816) is a large, beautiful shrine not far from Tokuyama Station. It dates back around thirteen hundred years, and the current green-roofed structure is a beautiful example of old Suo architecture. It has a modern banquet facility as well, where it hosts weddings, formal dinners, and even the occasional sake event. **Yamasaki Hachimangu** (1-9-10 Miyanomae, Shunan 746-0017) in the Shinnan'yo district is another shrine with more than a thousand years of history. Its grounds are filled with cherry and maple trees, creating pink springs and crimson autumns.

Those who have some Japanese-language skill would do well to visit the Shunan tourist information office **Machi no Port** まちのポート outside the Miyako Gate of Tokuyama Station for local events and other tourist information. Machi no Port occasionally teams up with the three Shunan breweries for sake tastings and similar events. It also has their sake for sale and sometimes even offers tasting flights from the three Shunan sake breweries on select days.

Hanaoka Hachimangu shrine (400 Suetakekami, Kudamatsu 744-0024) is the most important historic site in Kudamatsu. Found to the north of the route 188 bypass near Suohanaoka Station, it is in an old residential neighborhood with very narrow streets and poor access, but those with the means to get there really should try. This shrine goes back over thirteen hundred years and was historically a place where Shinto and Buddhism mixed, with temples and shrines sharing the same grounds. The **Akaibo-toba** tower on the grounds is a registered National Important Cultural Property and holds many historical treasures. The spring water used in the *temizuya* basin at the entrance, where visitors wash their hands and mouths before entering, also feeds a stream that provides the brewing water for Kinfundo, Kudamatsu's sole sake brewery, which is adjacent to the shrine.

Drinking Shunan

The area outside of Tokuyama Station's north, or Miyako, entrance is lined with restaurants and izakaya (casual evening restaurants focusing on drinking) featuring various local sake labels. Of particular note is **Densuke Honten** (2-9-5 Shinmachi, Shunan 745-0017), which focuses on *oden*, a dish featuring various treats like boiled egg, daikon radish, or tofu slow-simmered in a rich broth. I also recommend **Akaoni Bunten** (2-28-2 Heiwadori, Shunan 745-0015) for its take on the Yamaguchi specialty of stir-fried *chasoba* noodles topped with egg and beef. The manager of Akaoni Bunten is the former head of Shunan's late great sake bar Kokushu, Kawashima Keiji, who brings his love of great drink to this new evening dining spot.

YAMAGUCHI CITY

The most famous, and rightly so, of Yamaguchi City's sights is **Ruriko-ji temple** (7-1 Kozancho, Yamaguchi 753-0081) and its five-storied pagoda. The tower dates back to 1442 and is a listed National Treasure of Japan. Experts in such things rate it as one of the three best examples of such towers in Japan, alongside Horyu-ji temple tower in Nara and Daigo-ji temple's in Kyoto. The tower is surrounded by beautiful **Kozan Park** (7-1 Kozancho, Yamaguchi 753-0081), which has several other temple buildings and a small museum dedicated to all things pagoda.

Another sight in the park is **Chinryutei teahouse**. Saigo

The Joei-ji temple and Sesshu-tei garden in Yamaguchi City

Takamori, one of the key figures of the Meiji Restoration, came here with his acolytes to, supposedly, study the art of tea. They were actually plotting the overthrow of the shogun—and since they succeeded, this is now a site of great historical import.

St. Francis Xavier Memorial Church (4-1B Kameyamacho, Yamaguchi 753-0089) is open to the public for tours (9:00 to 17:00 every day) and has a small museum (closed on Wednesdays, ¥300 admission) on the first floor dedicated to the history of Christianity in Japan. The church is thoroughly modern, as the current structure only dates back to 1998, but the museum is most certainly of deep historical interest.

Joei-ji temple (2001 Miyanoshimo, Yamaguchi 753-0011) is a Zen temple some five hundred years old and is of particular interest for its garden, named **Sesshu-tei** (8:00 to 17:00; closes 16:30 November to March, ¥300 admission). As you might expect from the name, it was designed by famed artist Sesshu (1420–1506), who visited Yamaguchi under invitation from Ouchi Masahiro, who had also sponsored the artist's visits to China to study. It is a lovely example of Muromachi-period (1333–1573) Japanese gardens and is open to the public for walks and quiet contemplation.

Drinking Yamaguchi City

Yamaguchi City is overflowing with wonderful restaurants serving local sake, particularly in the hot-spring town of Yuda Onsen. One of the most popular is **Isokura** (4-2-31 Yudaonsen 753-0056), a grilled-food focused izakaya with a wonderfully extensive menu of local labels.

Yuda Onsen is also home to one of Yamaguchi Prefecture's most well-stocked sake shops, **Harada Shuho** (1-11-23 Yuda-onsen 753-0056). Just a few meters down and across the street is the tourist office, hot spring foot-bath, and café **Kitsune no Ashiato** (2 -1-3 Yudaonsen 753-0056), which also offers a great selection of local brands in tasting flights.

HOFU

Hofu became the seat of power of the Mori clan in Suo in 1600 when they replaced the Ouchi clan as rulers of the provinces Suo no Kuni and Nagato no Kuni. The main capital was in Hagi, but Hofu remained an important city, and there are plenty of living reminders of that history. **Hofu Tenmangu shrine** (14-1 Matsu-zakicho, Hofu 747-0029, open 9:00 to 16:00, ¥500 admission) is one of the most prominent shrines dedicated to Tenjin, the *kami* (god) of education, as well as the oldest, dating back to 904. An exquisite structure, it serves as the metaphorical heart of the city and is a testament to the prosperity that Hofu enjoyed under Mori patronage.

Suo Kokubun-ji temple (2-67 Kokubunjicho, Hofu 747-0021, open 9:00 to 16:00, ¥500 admission) dates back to 741 and is one of sixty-eight Kokubunji (or state-owned) temples built by Emperor

Shomu. It is possibly the only one that still exists in its original location, as most were either destroyed or moved in the thirteen hundred years since they were built. The main hall, rebuilt in the late eighteenth century atop the original temple's location, is filled with highly valuable statuary and artifacts. Several of the existing buildings were built by the Mori lords and stand as evidence of their power and the extent to which their mark has been preserved on local history.

Another remnant of that history is **Mori-shi Teien Garden** (1-15-1 Tatara, Hofu 747-0023), a sprawling park in the city center that was the private residence of the Mori clan elites after the Meiji Restoration. The manor house has been converted to a museum filled with national treasures and historical documents. The manor's main gate and wall also remain, and the perfectly maintained grounds within offer rolling scenery that seems out of time itself. The separate garden is one of the most beautiful in Yamaguchi, and well worth the time and trouble of getting there. The park is free to wander, but access to the museum and its attached garden requires a ticket (open 9:00 to 17:00, ¥1,200 yen for double access, ¥1,000 for museum only).

> **Drinking Hofu**
> **Kyoryoriya Shinto** (1-1-25 Midorimachi, Hofu 747-0026) is a *kaiseki ryori* restaurant, meaning it features the kind of elegant small-dish multi-course meals that Kyoto is known for. The cuisine is matched by an ever-shifting selection of exceptional sake and shochu, including of course a wide range of local favorites.

SHIMONOSEKI

Shimonoseki is one of Yamaguchi's most tourist-oriented cities. The shinkansen station is convenient to a major mall, a small amusement park, and **Kaikyokan** aquarium (6-1 Arukapoto, Shimonoseki

750-0036). The aquarium is right on the Kanmon Straits, and in addition to the usual dolphin and penguin shows, it has extensive exhibits of local sea creatures.

Karato Ichiba fish market (5-50 Karato, Shimonoseki 750-0005) is another classic Shimonoseki attraction. It is a bustling market with daily auctions of fresh-caught seafood. The local waters are one of the largest sources of prized fugu blowfish in Japan, and you will see mascots, pictures, and statues of the fish all over town. You can enjoy the freshest sushi (sometimes still moving!) at stalls inside the market, while the surrounding boardwalk is full of shops and restaurants of all sorts. A direct bus to the market leaves from right outside Shimonoseki Station.

If you can time it right, the Shimonoseki Straits Festival on May 3 is quite the spectacle. It commemorates the ending of the Genpei War (1185) in a fierce naval battle here, complete with boats reenacting the battle on the strait. The highlight is a grand procession of people dressed as courtiers visiting **Akama Shrine** (4-1 Amidaijicho, Shimonoseki 750-0003) facing the straits.

Upscale izakaya **Ren** has various locations around Shimonoseki, but the main shop (2-3-7 Akine Nishimachi, Shimonoseki 751-0873) inside Shinshimonoseki Quest is directly connected to Shin-Shimonoseki Station. Its menu, made up of creative takes on usual izakaya fare, like fried cheese mixed with crushed wild yam or seasonal salads with locally caught sashimi, is perfect for snacking and dining along with local sake favorites like Taka or Toyobijin.

Drinking Shimonoseki

Restaurant **Tonogawa** (1-17 Chofunakahamacho, Shimonoseki 752-0975) is on the east side of the city, along the seaside. It offers a wide variety of seafood, including the city's famous fugu (blowfish) served any number of ways, and boasts one of the prefecture's largest sake lists. The selection of local sake is extensive, and also seasonal, so fall *hiyaoroshi* (sake pressed in spring, pasteurized once, then aged over the summer) or winter *hatsushibori* (the very first pressing of the brewing season, often sold unpasteurized) are something to look out for.

SAN'YO-ONODA

There is, sadly, not a lot of tourist infrastructure in San'yo-Onoda. If you have a car you can get out of town to visit lovely **Ryuozan Park** (1261 Banyadake, Onoda, San'yo-Onoda 756-0817) and enjoy a view of the sunset or a lovely nature walk through **Ejio Park** (401-1 Takahata, San'yo Onoda 756-0021). Both are overflowing with cherry blossoms in the early spring.

Train travelers are limited to exploring the city areas on foot. Walking around Nagayama Shuzo's Asa area will get you a nice glimpse of small-town Japan, but not a whole lot else.

Drinking San'yo-Onoda

Izakaya **Ikoi no Ba** (1-3-2 Asa, San'yo-Onoda 757-0001) in front of Asa Station offers up standard izakaya fare (yakitori, fried rice, potstickers) and local treats like fried fugu blowfish and Yamaguchi's own breed of chicken, *choshudori* in all kinds of dishes, but the real show is a near-complete lineup of Yamazaru from neighborhood brewery Nagayama Shuzo. Other Yamaguchi breweries are represented as well.

MINE

Mine is prime territory for nature tourism. The quasi-national park at **Akiyoshidai Plateau** is perfect for casual walks or longer hikes through the limestone-dotted landscape. The entrance to **Akiyoshido** cave, which runs beneath it, is near the park, and the walk within is a blessed cooldown in summer. Both of these are

The Akiyoshidai Plateau's limestone-dotted lanscape

accessible by bus from major train stations in the area, but if you
have a car head for **Kagekiyodo** cave at Akiyoshidai Auto Camping
Ground (3108 Mitochoaka, Mine 754-0302). You can take an easy
stroll into the cool, beautiful cave interior, but the second half of
the cave remains dark and unpaved for explorers to venture into
with flashlight, helmet, and rubber boots (available for rent at the
entrance).

Another beautiful sight in Mine is **Beppu Benten Ike** pond (482
Shuhocho Beppu, Mine 754-0603), the spring-fed pond that provides Ohmine Shuzo with its water. The pond is a brilliant blue-
green, and nearby faucets offer its clean, cold water to people for
filling their jugs and bottles. There is also a trout farm here, and you
can dine on the fresh-caught fish at the restaurant on-site or try
catching your own to cook yourself.

UBE

Ube's primary offering is industrial landscape. The waterfront is
lined with chemical plants, glass factories, and other facilities that
create a maze of pipes, conveyor belts, and smokestacks. It is an

aesthetically interesting sight, if a bit more *Blade Runner*–esque than you might expect from a small Japanese city.

There are, however, pleasant areas to explore. **Tokiwa Park**, (3-4-1 Norisada, Ube 755-0003) is out near the airport on the southeast part of town and has a wide lake with pedal boats and an attached amusement park and zoo (both small and aging). There is a botanical garden in the park as well and a concentration of open-air sculpture and art installations to wander through.

Sorin-ji temple (210 Kogushi, Ube 755-0067) is a small Zen temple with a beautiful garden. The temple is a quiet space and offers zazen sessions, but the garden is the biggest draw. Named Ryushin-tei and dating back to the 1300s, it is the oldest Zen garden in Yamaguchi and uses a very rare design that incorporates the scenery of the mountain ridge in the background into the view of the central pond with its spread of pebbles recreating a tidal flat. There is a small fee to walk the garden.

Kotozaki Hachimangu shrine (571 Kamiube, Ube 755-0091) is a large, beautiful shrine that is a relatively easy walk from Kotoshiba Station on the Ube Line. It has achieved some notoriety for selling *omamori* charms, small decorated amulets believed to offer all kinds of luck and protection. Here you can choose from eight hundred different varieties! The scenery and architecture are beautiful as well.

Drinking Ube

Ube's Shintencho is a covered shopping arcade a bit of a walk from Ube Shinkawa Station but home to one of the most attractive sake bars in the prefecture: **Nihonshu Bar Niichan no Mise** (1-2-35 Shintencho, Ube 755-0029). Niichan means "big brother," and the owner/bartender here just happens to be Nagayama Masayuki, older brother to Nagayama Takahiro of Nagayama Honke Shuzo—Ube's only sake brewery. The bar stocks sake from nearly all of Yamaguchi's sake breweries, and as Masayuki once headed up his family brewery's sales department, he knows the industry inside and out. His taste can be trusted! The bar also has a food menu.

ABU/HAGI

The small town of Abu is home to delicious produce and a few beautiful spots. **Michi-no-Eki Abucho** (2249 Nago, Abu 759-3622) is just the place to visit if you'd like to try the fruits of Abu's fields and seas. The location is best reached by driving, of course, but is not out of walking distance from Nago Station on the San'in Main Line.

Reaching Hagi can also be a bit of a trek. It is on the San'in Main Line, too, but shinkansen travelers should best take one of the many Bocho or JR shuttle buses from Shin-Yamaguchi station in Yamaguchi City. The quickest option is the Hagi-go Bus shuttle that runs nonstop from the station and takes about one hour.

Hagi works hard to preserve its historic heritage. Although the castle is gone, its grounds and outer wall remain, and the surrounding castle town district retains a number of samurai manses, old white yard walls, and beautiful gardens. There are a number of World Heritage sites around Hagi connected to the Meiji Restoration, including the castle ruins and the old castle town, **Hagi Reverberatory Furnace** (4897-7 Chinto, Hagi 758-0011), and **Shokasonjuku Academy** (viewable on the grounds of Shoin shrine, 1537 Chinto, Hagi 758-0011) where Yoshida Shoin taught military arts and politics to the future leaders of Japan.

The legacy of old Hagi extends beyond architecture. Hagi is the focus of one of Japan's most valued tea-ware pottery styles, Hagi-yaki. The porous clay and delicately crazed glazing on this style of pottery has earned it a reputation as one of Japan's three most desired styles for traditional tea ceremonies (See "Connections: Ceramic Artists").

Hagi has many museums, of course. **Hagi Uragami Museum** (586-1 Hiyakomachi, Hagi 758-0074, open 9:00 to 17:00, closed Mondays, ¥300 admission) displays the collection of Hagi-born businessman Uragami Toshiro. It has over five thousand ukiyo-e prints, five hundred pieces of ancient Chinese and Korean pottery, and many more modern pieces as well. **Hagi Meiringakusha** (602 Emukai, Hagi 758-0041, open 9:00 to 17:00, closed the first Tuesday and Wednesday in February, ¥300 admission) is a museum dedicated to the history of the city, focusing on its central role in the Meiji Restoration, and is located in a building that was once an Edo-period school for the nobility. There is extensive English support available. **Hagi Museum** (355 Horiuchi, Hagi 758-0057, open 9:00 to 17:00, unfixed closed days, ¥520 admission) is a more general museum, with exhibits on nature and science, as well as local history.

Travel around Hagi is made relatively easy using the official loop bus that tours all the points of interest in the city in two circuits; each ride costs ¥100. Bus passes are available at various locations around town, including tourist offices.

Drinking Hagi

Sake and wine specialist shop **SAKAYA** (522-1 Hijiwara, Hagi 758-0025) not only has an enormous bottle selection but their second floor *kaku-uchi* (tasting) area sells by the glass. The list of local brands is impressive, and there is a great range of national labels as well. The elegant atmosphere here is perfect for a quiet moment of sake-fueled contemplation.

Afterword

I began working on this book around March 2020, just as the Covid-19 pandemic was becoming a real thing. I had been using my meager skills to help support the local sake industry that I loved by writing magazine articles about breweries and translating websites, catalogs, and whatnot, but I soon felt that I was missing a bigger picture. Sake is made by individuals, but those individuals do not exist in a vacuum. They are part of a community, or many communities, and that shapes their sake as much as anything.

So, rather than approaching the local brewing scene piecemeal, I felt it was time to approach it as a whole—to investigate the web of breweries, farmers, retailers, consumers, and all the other many pieces that make up the culture of sake and to set sake within its culture as a whole. I also, I must admit, wanted an excuse to visit every one of these breweries to get a sense of their identity myself.

As the pandemic progressed, and as the sake industry began to suffer in earnest, my work took on another flavor—one of documentation. I began to sense that some of these breweries might not survive the enormous economic hardships caused by restrictions on dining and drinking. I wanted to record these people and their work, because they might not be there for much longer.

Luckily, at the time of this writing. with all of my visits and interviews finished, none of Yamaguchi's breweries have fallen to the virus. Things are bad, and not getting much better, but the flexibility and resilience that helped bring the Yamaguchi Sake Revolution to bear have also kept these small local breweries afloat. No one, of course, knows what tomorrow will bring, but for today, the nectar still flows.

Acknowledgments

This book would not have been possible without the help of many, many people.

I would like to offer particular thanks to:

Yamagata Toshiro in his role as the head of the Yamaguchi Sake Brewers Association, who encouraged and aided me at every turn.

Brian Ashcraft, Arline Lyons, Andrew Russell, and Matt Trayvaud for their invaluable advice and critiques of my early drafts and proposals, and for putting up with all kinds of silliness on Twitter.

My wife and son for being the reason for getting out of bed every day, and for desperately wanting to get some sleep every night. In particular, my wife was instrumental in helping make sure my Japanese emails weren't inexcusably rude.

My friend Kono Tomoyuki for driving me all over the darned place.

Simone Maynard and the whole Taste with the Toji crew for all the wonderful opportunities they bring to sake, and to me.

And, of course, all of the brewery kuramoto, toji, and staff who welcomed me into their spaces, answered all my questions, and helped me do this.

Tasting Notes